A VOICE FROM THE MONASTERY

LISTEN WITH YOUR HEART

*Deepen Your Spiritual Life
with the Rule of Saint Benedict*

M. Basil Pennington, OCSO
EDITED BY Brother Chaminade Crabtree, OCSO

PARACLETE PRESS
BREWSTER, MASSACHUSETTS

Listen with Your Heart:
Deepen Your Spiritual Life with the Rule of Saint Benedict

2007   First Printing

Copyright © 2007 by Our Lady of the Holy Spirit Monastery

ISBN: 978-1-55725-548-8

Selections from *The Rule of Saint Benedict, In Latin and English with Notes*, edited by Timothy Fry, OSB, Copyright © 1981 by The Order of St. Benedict, Inc. Published by The Liturgical Press, Collegeville, Minnesota. Reprinted with permission.

Except where noted, all biblical quotations are from the New American Bible (© 1970 Old Testament with 1986 Revised New Testament by the Confraternity of Christian Doctrine, Washington, D.C.)

Library of Congress Cataloging-in-Publication Data
Pennington, M. Basil.
  Listen with your heart : deepen your spiritual life with the rule of Saint Benedict / M. Basil Pennington ; edited by Brother Chaminade Crabtree.
      p. cm.
  Includes bibliographical references.
  ISBN-13: 978-1-55725-548-8
  1. Benedict, Saint, Abbot of Monte Cassino. Regula. 2. Spiritual life--Christianity. I. Crabtree, Chaminade. II. Title.
  BX3004.Z5P46 2007
  255'.106--dc22   2007014787

Published by Paraclete Press
Brewster, Massachusetts
www.paracletepress.com

Printed in the United States of America

CONTENTS

# FOREWORD

I count it a joy and privilege to be asked to write a foreword for Father Basil Pennington's book, *Listen with Your Heart*, based on the teachings of the Rule of St. Benedict. As a Baptist preacher, pastor, and seminary adjunct professor, I had the honor of meeting Father Basil when he was installed as the abbot at Our Lady of the Holy Spirit Monastery at Conyers, Georgia in 2000. He was a charismatic, John Wayne-like figure who possessed a deep reverence for God, the universal church, and a child-like spirit for prayer and worship. I remember him as a "gentle giant" in stature and in spirit!

In 2001, I was invited to join an interdenominational group of Christians who met at the Monastery of the Holy Spirit to attend a week-long spirituality discovery with the Masters Foundation, of which Abbot Basil was a founding member. Basil served as our guest lecturer and prayer facilitator. The core of our prayers dealt with learning how to do "centering prayer" and how to develop a personal declaration for living out our faith. That week, Basil pressed me to declare, "I am a conduit of God's grace!" Amazingly, I still use that declaration today. It informs all that I do. Basil was masterful in his teaching and modeling how to do contemplative praying. I was mesmerized at how quickly he could quiet his spirit as he demonstrated the use of techniques for centering prayer. When he returned from centering prayer, his deep, baritone voice was soothing and deliberate. I quickly became a fan of centering prayer and have used it at home, church office, busy airport waiting areas, in my leadership development consulting and counseling, and of course, at the Monastery where I frequently go on retreat.

I am a true Pennington fan and am amazed at how simple he was always able to communicate the gospel in his teaching and modeling! You will find his style to be deeply spiritual, biblically sound, culturally relevant, and adaptive to many Christian settings. Basil writes and speaks from a perspective of a seasoned Christian grandfather who had many spiritual "children." You will be inspired, informed, challenged, and connected to a God who patiently waits to be alone with us in prayer.

Basil's ministry touched many people: male and female, children and adults, Catholics and Protestants. I am deeply grateful to Brother Chaminade and Paraclete Press who had the vision and commitment to publish these teachings of Basil on the Rule. Though Basil's death occurred before this publication, God is such an awesome God to resurrect Basil's vision for a book like this from the grave! I highly recommend it to anyone looking to grow spiritually. Catholics as well as Protestant pastors, teachers, and lay-leaders can greatly benefit from its teachings, truths and discipline. As you read this profound reflection, may you truly listen to God with all of your heart! Shalom in Jesus, Father M. Basil Pennington!

Rev. Dr. Kenneth R. Board, Pastor
Pilgrim Baptist Church
Rockford, Illinois

INTRODUCTION

Father M. Basil Pennington was elected abbot of Our Lady of the Holy Spirit Monastery on August 4, 2000. "I thought I retired," he joked with us at his first meeting. He was sixty-nine years old and had spent forty-five years teaching and writing about the Cistercian heritage of contemplation and prayer. He became a well-known author through his books on centering prayer (or "prayer of the heart"). He helped found Cistercian Publications to increase the availability of English translations of early Cistercian writings. For decades he wrote a weekly column for the *Brooklyn Tablet*, his hometown diocesan newspaper. For several years he helped the monks at Lantao, China, stabilize their community. At the time of his election, he was the appointed superior of Assumption Abbey in Missouri, in what he thought would be his last service to the order before returning to his home monastery of St. Joseph's Abbey in Spencer, Massachusetts. However, the abbacy awaited him at a monastery in Georgia.

Abbot Basil's life was one of service. He wished to serve others through his calling as monk, priest, and abbot. He told us monks, "I want to serve you as your abbot with all my heart, all my strength, and all my soul." And he did. Abbot Basil was a shepherd of his monastic flock. The care of the elder monks at Conyers was his primary concern. The monks who had devoted themselves to the construction of the monastery during the 1950s were now aged and needed not only physical care but the facilities for it. Abbot Basil saw to it that they had what was needed. He raised the money for a new elevator so the monks could attend daily Mass and the Divine Office in the monastery church. Having spread the charism of contemplative prayer through his books, Abbot Basil began prayer retreats in the monastery's retreat house. Additional retreats on subjects such as Scripture and *lectio divina* were added to the list. The financial stability of the monastery was one of his concerns as well: a fruitcake business was soon started. Abbot Basil had a vision of monastic life and worked to bring it into reality.

Twice a week, Abbot Basil addressed the monks. In the Sunday address, known as a chapter talk, he would speak on various monastic topics that would aid the community in growth. Conversion of manners was the aim—that is, one's growth as a Christian. His Thursday talks were on the Rule of Saint Benedict for monks. And that is the subject of this book.

Benedict of Nursia's Rule, written in the sixth century, is a guiding document for monks who wish to live according to Jesus Christ's gospel. For Abbot Basil, it was important for monks to know the Rule well and to live it faithfully in the modern context. Using his monastic experience of living the Rule and his study of it, Abbot Basil spoke with his usual enthusiasm. His talks were recorded on cassettes, a standard practice to allow for later listening by absent monks.

For most of Abbot Basil's two and a half years as abbot, I was his secretary. It was a challenge to keep up with him. Keeping track of the voluminous letters from readers of his books, taking phone messages, and recording the minutes of meetings kept me busy. Yet, there were cherished moments with Abbot Basil, especially in the morning when he would plan his day and assign me tasks. We spoke of things other than work, however, and I would get a glimpse of his immense love for the Church.

Abbot Basil wanted to share the Cistercian heritage with others, so he wrote about it in articles and books, preached it in his homilies, and spoke about it in his talks to monks and retreatants. He told me that he had always wanted to write a commentary on Saint Benedict's Rule, but he had just never gotten around to doing so. Now, all he could do was give talks on the Rule. He never wrote his talks, but seemed to speak fluently from a mental outline. Perhaps this is a good place to inform the reader that I have tried to keep his talks much in the style in which they were given—as speech and not that of writing. Basil recited Scripture verses from memory. He did not intend his Scripture references to be exact readings from any one translation. When his own Scripture recitations occur, I have used "cf"—meaning "compare" to the actual Scripture.

Abbot Basil resigned from the abbatial office in late April 2002. It was time for the monastery he loved to continue with leadership from within. Abbot Basil's resignation was sudden but necessary for the monks to take ownership of their future.

Returning to Spencer Abbey in Massachusetts, Abbot Basil continued to pray and write. He had a number of works in progress. I kept in contact with him and asked him one day about his commentary on the Rule. "Oh, yes," he laughed. "It's on the list."

In March 2005, Abbot Basil was in a serious car accident. He never recovered, and he died on June 3. I grieved his death. He had done much for me personally. I was consecrated a solemnly professed monk by him shortly before his resignation. He still had much to offer the Cistercian Order through his writing and mere presence in a world in need of prayer. I thought about him each day when a passage from Benedict's Rule was read after our community dinner. It finally struck me that the commentary on the Rule he had always wanted to write was already written. So I set about transcribing his talks on the Rule and posted them on our monastery's website. Editor Jon Sweeney of Paraclete Press, a close friend of Abbot Basil, came across the talks and approached me about putting them into a book. Thanks to Jon's encouragement, Abbot Basil's commentary on Benedict's Rule is now a reality—or at least a partial commentary. Abbot Basil never covered the entire Rule: he began with the prologue and then spoke about select chapters.

Commentaries and studies have already been written on Benedict's Rule. Does Abbot Basil present anything new? I think the answer to this question depends on you, the reader. Put yourself in a room full of monks with their abbot—a towering figure—at the head. Be attentive "with the ear of your heart," as Benedict says in the first sentence of his prologue. Allow the Spirit to speak to you through the abbot's words. Allow Abbot Basil to continue his service to us through his words of wisdom.

In one short talk that Abbot Basil gave on the Rule—a talk that is not included here in full as it consisted mostly of our abbot asking us to prepare for our annual retreat— he asked something of us that has similar application for every Christian. Here is what he said:

> We have to look at ourselves. When Bernard was a novice and struggled, he always kept asking himself, *Ad quid venisti.* "What do you seek?" Or, "For what have I come?" I think we have to ask those questions all of our lives. For what have I come? We want to go

back and ask, Why did I come to the monastery in the first place? What was I looking for? What was enticing me to this life? Have I kept that hope green? Does that hope really live in me now as it lived in me when I first came here? Is that hope big enough? In a way that hope should be much greater now than it ever was before, because *He who eats of me will hunger still, he who drinks of me will thirst for more* (Sir. 24:20). The more we receive, the more we should have: the more sense of the fullness that we are called to as sons of God, of men [or women] divinized in the divinity of Christ.

I'm sure that Abbot Basil would want me to say that all who read this should ask themselves similar questions.

Brother Chaminade Crabtree, ocso
Our Lady of the Holy Spirit Monastery
Conyers, Georgia

I ❧ BELOVED CHILDREN OF GOD

[1]Listen carefully, my son, to the master's instructions, and attend to them with the ear of your heart. This is advice from a father who loves you; welcome it, and faithfully put it into practice. [2]The labor of obedience will bring you back to him from whom you had drifted through the sloth of disobedience. [3]This message of mine is for you, then, if you are ready to give up your own will, once and for all, and armed with the strong and noble weapons of obedience to do battle for the true King, Christ the Lord.

—Prologue
THE RULE OF SAINT BENEDICT

Obsculta, fili or *Obsculta, o fili,* Saint Benedict says.[1] Most translations mistranslate that. Usually the translations say, "Listen, my son." That is not what Saint Benedict said. He said "Listen, O son." He is speaking to us precisely in our dignity and reality as sons. We have been baptized into Christ, raised up to be sharers in the divine nature and life. It is precisely in sharing the sonship of Christ that we find our true dignity, our true reality. We are sons of God.

Knowing God as Father. Speaking about listening, we mention many times that we are all a certain listening, a certain openness to reality which has been shaped and formed by the whole of our lifetime experience. We each have a certain listening. That is why it can be so valuable when we sit together to share and discuss; each of us brings his own listening to it—what he has heard—so that we arrive at a fuller understanding of reality.

Each of us certainly has his own particular listening for the sonship. Each of us knows ourselves as a son, and each of us knows this in relation to our father. We bring this over into our relationship with God. We tend very much to see our relationship with God our Father as colored by our experience of our relationship with our own fathers—whether it be our natural father, our adopted father, our stepfather, and so on. This all colors that relationship we have with God the Father.

Jesus says, *What father among you would hand his son a snake when he asks for a fish? Or hand him a scorpion when he asks for an egg? If you then, who are wicked, know how to give good gifts to your children, how much more will the Father in heaven give the Holy Spirit to those who ask him?* (Lk. 11:11–13). Jesus uses the natural goodness that is in the father, that we have all experienced in varying degrees as children, as a step—an entrance—into an understanding of the goodness of God our Father. Yet, it is very limited. All of us are not only poor, weak, stupid sinners, but our fathers are also poor, weak, stupid sinners!

Part of coming to real maturity as men is to be able to accept this fact: our fathers and our mothers were, like ourselves, poor, weak, stupid sinners. We idolize our parents, so one of the shattering experiences of life is oftentimes when we come to find that they have their weaknesses, sins, faults, and failures, too. Our maturity is in being able to respect them and love them as the source of our life and be grateful for that, but fully accept them in that reality of their weaknesses and sinfulness. Because we are all poor, weak, stupid sinners, we are a very poor image of God.

THE PRODIGAL SON

Saint Paul says, in his turn, that all paternity comes down from heaven, from the Father of Lights (Eph. 3:15–16). God is the supreme archetype of paternity—his total, complete, gratuitous giving of self. It is that paternity we want to come to understand, and to understand ourselves as sons in relation to that paternity. The more insight we have into ourselves as sons, and how that has been affected by our experience of sonship and fathership in our relationship with our own fathers—our natural fathers, or stepfathers, and so on—the more we can be aware of our need to understand and be healed by an understanding and experience of the sonship that is in Christ Jesus: the sonship which Jesus reveals in the Gospels, and the fatherhood of God that Jesus also reveals in the Gospels.

We search the Gospels to understand more and more fully what it means to be a son. *This is my beloved son, with whom I am well pleased* (Mt. 17:5). And what it means to be a son of that Father. *I always do what is pleasing to him* (Jn. 8:29). There is no doubt that as our father Saint Benedict speaks here of sonship, he has in mind our Lord's story of the Prodigal Son. This story is one of the great insightful stories of the Gospels, where Jesus tries to bring us—who know ourselves as poor, weak, stupid, sinful sons—into the reality of the relationship.

Saint Benedict says:

Listen, carefully, my son, to the master's instructions, and attend to them with the ear of your heart. This is advice from a father who loves you; welcome it, and faithfully put it into practice. The labor of obedience will bring you back to him from whom you had drifted through the sloth of disobedience.[2]

The journey of the Prodigal Son back to God is a return from the "land of unlikeness," as Saint Bernard would say in the Cistercian school.[3] We have always had the image of God (Gen. 1:27; 9:6). We are made in the image of God—of God the Son, Jesus. We were originally made in the image and likeness of God, but we lost that likeness and went into the land of unlikeness. We are coming back to that. It is the return of the Prodigal Son.

THE WITNESS OF HENRI NOUWEN

I had a wonderful friend in a man whom you all undoubtedly are familiar with in one way or another—Henri Nouwen.[4] Henri was a full professor at Yale for ten years, and he used to come regularly to Spencer Abbey. Later, he was a professor at Harvard. Henri, in the minds of many people, had reached the pinnacle there. What more prestigious position can you have than as a full professor at Yale and Harvard? There aren't many people who manage that. Yet, Henri was always a tortured man. He wrote his classic work about the "wounded healer" because he was doing a tremendous work of healing.[5] He was conscious of himself as a wounded person and struggled with this all his life. It was only in a short time before his death that he finally came to peace, and it was precisely through the experience of the Prodigal Son. He knew that Gospel. He had read it many times and preached on it. One day, as he was looking upon the painting of the Prodigal Son by Rembrandt, he knew he was the Prodigal Son and what that meant. It changed his life; it completed his life. He wrote that wonderful book on it.[6] He was actually on his way to St. Petersburg [Russia] to do a video in the presence of that picture when—by God's mercy, he had returned home, and for the first time was with his family in peace and joy—God called him to himself. His life was complete.

EPIPHANY MOMENTS IN OUR LIVES

That is a powerful word that the Lord gives us in the parable of the Prodigal Son. We all know ourselves to be the Prodigal Son, and we are on that journey. We are at different places on the journey, but there is a significant moment on the journey—a moment of epiphany.

An epiphany is an important moment in our lives. It is the moment when we finally see. As the senior monks could tell you, the Epiphany was one of the great feasts of the year. It was a sermon major with a full octave, like Christmas, Easter, and Pentecost. Why is the Epiphany such a great feast? It is the feast of the experience, the manifestation of the wondrous mystery that God actually became man. God sent his Son to save us. God the Father sacrificed his supreme Son—his perfect Son—to save us poor, stupid, sinful sons. It is when we have that epiphany—when we come to really know by a divine manifestation what the reality is—then truly do we live.

The Prodigal Son returning home had his whole plan of how this was going to work out. It looked like a beautiful and a good plan. I am going to go and prostrate before my father. I am going to kiss his feet, and I am going to say, "Father, I'm not worthy to be your son. Make me a hired servant. I'll work for you the rest of my life!" He had to completely give up his own plan and accept the father's plan.

That story, as Jesus told it, was absolutely shocking to his hearers. It was a patriarchal society. The father was it! He had power of life and death over all his children and over all his servants. He was the one whom people *did* come to and kiss his feet. In our own context, the older monks can remember how the abbot used to be: You came to him, you made a profound bow, you kneeled down and kissed his ring. You could never imagine the abbot as being the guy in the kitchen washing the dishes. It was the patriarchal society. The idea of a father picking up his robe, running out and embracing this smelly little brat who had betrayed him and threw away his heritage was just absolutely incomprehensible to these people.

DROPPING OUR PLANS
AND ACCEPTING THE FATHER'S WAY

What that Prodigal Son had to accept at that moment was to drop his own plan completely and accept the father's embrace of love. Accept the father's way. Let the father clothe him in the new garment—the garment we receive when we receive the habit. Put on his finger a ring, a pledge of a relationship as deep as the marital relation. Celebrate him! Kill the fatted calf!

I would venture to say that this is precisely that deep struggle each one of us is having. To be able to move out of our own plan and our own self-identity—a false self, even though it is a self that has a lot of truth in it—and see ourselves as poor, weak, stupid sinners. Being able to step out of that and accept the reality of who we are: the beloved son of God who is love beyond anything we can comprehend. And let God celebrate us! We all struggle with that. The only way we are going to make the breakthrough is when we have the experience—which we only have in contemplative prayer—when we experience God actually saying to us, "This is my son, my beloved, in whom I am well pleased" (cf. Mt. 17:5). When we have that experience, then we are completely freed and can know ourselves as the beloved child of God.

Even though we are poor, weak, stupid sinners, we are the beloved child of God whom he celebrates (1 Jn. 3:2). We do not stand anymore in self-righteousness like the good boy who stayed home and did everything his father always wanted. No. We do not get crushed down by our stupid sinfulness, but we accept the reality that we are embraced with divine love. We are God's beloved sons! That's the thing to truly seek.

We should ask ourselves: How do I see myself as son and God as father and open myself to this conversion?

Then we will be ready for the epiphany of Easter, when we will truly know that we have been baptized into the risen Christ, that we are the beloved son who has the fullness of eternal life. We have overcome the sin of death.

CONSIDERING THE COST

Why do we hold back from this? Because we know it is going to cost. It is going to cost us to be profoundly humble. To know our true dignity, to know God's fantastic love, and to know our poor, weak, stupid sinfulness is profoundly humbling. It utterly destroys any shred of dignity we try to build up with the false self. And it calls us forth to live as sons. That is why our father Benedict says, "The labor of our obedience will bring us back to him from whom we have drifted through the sloth of disobedience."[7]

When we know our dignity, know who we truly are, know who God truly is, then there is something deep in us that cries out as did Jesus, *I always do what is pleasing to him* (Jn. 8:29). This means a real dying to self—all our self-will, all our own ideas, all our way of doing it. We know that, but we do not want to pay that price. The price we pay for not doing it is that we deprive ourselves of knowing who we truly are and of living in the glory and joy of being the beloved son of God.

I tell you, my brothers, that there is absolutely nothing in this world—nothing that I can possibly conceive of—that is more wonderful than this: to know that you are God's beloved son. It is total liberation. It's wondrous and great. It's a fulfillment of all the desires for love that you could possibly have. Love beyond your conceiving.

William of St. Thierry has a wonderful little treatise on prayer. He ends the last paragraph rather ironically.

If, however, we give way completely to laziness and sloth and out of the depths of our ignorance cry to God as out of a dungeon and if we want to be heard even when we are not seeking the Blessed face of Him to whom we cry, and if we do not care whether He is angry or appeased when He gives us what we want, as long as we get it. Well, a man who prays like that must be content with what God gives. He does not know how to ask God for a great thing so it is nothing great he receives.[8]

Jesus says to us in the Gospel, *Ask and it will be given to you; seek and you will find* (Mt. 7:7). God will give us whatever we want, and William is saying, "You're pretty stupid to ask for anything less than God himself!" This epiphany and this manifestation is the experience of who we truly are as sons and, therefore, who truly God is as Father. This is the experience of reality. It is the experience that is completely transforming. It is the experience that Saint Benedict calls us to when he says we are to truly seek God.[9] It is what our life is all about.

During this Lent, let us get more in touch with ourselves as we see ourselves as sons. Let that be re-formed by the way Jesus reveals *son* to us in the Gospels, and then *father*. Let this transformation open us to that experience when we let go of all our own ideas of how we are to return to the Father and let the Father totally embrace us, lift us up, and celebrate us as his beloved sons.

MAY THE DIVINE ASSISTANCE AMEN
REMAIN WITH US ALWAYS

II ✤ LISTEN TO THE MASTER

¹Listen carefully, my son, to the master's instructions, and attend to them with the ear of your heart. This is advice from a father who loves you; welcome it, and faithfully put it into practice. ²The labor of obedience will bring you back to him from whom you had drifted through the sloth of disobedience. ³This message of mine is for you, then, if you are ready to give up your own will, once and for all, and armed with the strong and noble weapons of obedience to do battle for the true King, Christ the Lord.

—Prologue
THE RULE OF SAINT BENEDICT

I have been talking about our Holy Rule and what it means to us. As I mentioned, in a classical Latin document the author carefully chooses the first word or two words to capture what he feels is the essence of what he is going to say—what the document means. The words that our Father Benedict chose were *obsculta, o fili*— "Listen, son."

Last time, we were talking about that "son." Benedict sees us essentially as son in the same way that we see Jesus as son. Jesus is the son in the Holy Trinity. We are baptized into Christ and participate in the depth—in a wondrous way and far beyond anything we could conceive—of being sons. Sons of God. But also, Benedict is speaking about the attitude of the son. We find in Jesus, through the Gospels, this perfect son-attitude. *I always do what is pleasing to him* (Jn. 8:29). *I give praise to you, Father, Lord of heaven and earth, for although you have hidden these things from the wise and the learned you have revealed them to the childlike* (Mt. 11:25). *Not my will but yours be done* (Lk. 22:42). We come to grasp the full meaning of the son-attitude as we search the Gospels and listen in *lectio*. We find our true identity as men who have been baptized "son." This son-attitude is the attitude that Benedict wants us to bring to our hearing heart of the Rule, to our living of the Rule. "Listen, son."

What would he have us listen to? "Listen, son, to the precepts of the master." *Praecepta magistri*—precepts of the master. The commentators have debated on precisely who is the master that Benedict is speaking of there. Is he speaking of himself as master? Or, is he speaking of Christ? *You call me "teacher" and "master," and rightly so, for indeed I am* (Jn. 13:13). Therefore, when he speaks of the precepts of the master, is he talking about the Rule or is he talking about the Gospels?

I say that the commentators are debating on this but, to me, it seems like a false debate. It certainly was for our Cistercian Fathers; they saw no great distinction between the Rule and the Gospels. Rather, they saw that the Rule was the way we lived the Gospels. It was the expression of the Gospels which we embrace.

THE WITNESS OF RICHARD OF YORK

I do not know if you're familiar with Richard of York. He was a monk of York, and he was the leader of the group that founded Fountains Abbey. He is the Robert of Molesme of England. His story is similar to how Robert led the monks forth from Molesme to found Cîteaux.[10] Richard led the monks from York to establish Fountains, except there was bit more drama. There is a wonderful description of it by Thurstan of York. Richard would express what they wanted to do: "We must undertake with all our strength to observe by God's grace the true and age-old service of Blessed Father Benedict, or rather, the more ancient Gospel of Christ which precedes all vows and rules."[11]

Richard had a great devotion to Benedict and the Rule.

Whatever the blessed Benedict established, the whole of it was designed by the providence of Holy Spirit, so that nothing more useful, more happy or more holy could be conceived. Saint Benedict acknowledges as his own only those who live under a monastery under a rule and an abbot, so, venerable Father [speaking to the archbishop], if you will allow, we will hasten back to the purity of the Gospels, to evangelical perfection, and peace.[12]

He is constantly seeing the relationship between the Rule and the Gospels. Thurstan himself says of the Cistercians: "They faithfully undertook a renewal of the Holy Rule and a total living of it. Indeed, it is clearer than light that in their wonderful way of life the truth of the whole Gospel shines forth."[13] Again, Thurstan, speaking of founders of Fountains, says: "Men who were determined to correct their way of life according to the Rule of Saint Benedict or, rather, according to the truths of the Gospel."[14]

They saw the two—the Gospels and the Rule—almost as one. In a sense, we can look at the precepts of the master as expressing the evangelical teachings that are at the heart, center, and fullness of the Rule. Or, we can speak of the Rule itself with Benedict as the master of monastic wisdom.

It is amazing today how many people are looking to Benedict. Non-Catholics are writing commentaries on the Rule of Saint Benedict; Christian groups are having Benedictine experiences by living in community. They are looking to Benedict as a great man of monastic wisdom and the Holy Rule as the expression of that wisdom.

PRAECEPTA AND PSALM 119

Benedict chooses the word *praecepta*. "Precepts" would be the literal translation. I noticed in RB 1980[15] that *praecepta* is translated as "instructions." In the New American Bible, they translate Our Lord's use of the word *magistri* as "master" (Mt. 23:10). Master here does not mean something like a task master or a slave master, but a master of theology, a master of teaching. His authority comes primarily from the richness of the teaching, of the wisdom he has to teach and share. Not just that, but he has a certain authority. He is a master of this house; the master of this community. Obviously, Benedict is very conscious of the biblical overtones of the word *praecepta*.

As you know, Benedict in the Rule provides that we should pray Psalm 119 every week at the midday office— the office of Sext. The revelation is so beyond that it cannot be captured in simple conceptual language. "What eye has not seen, and ear has not heard, and what has not entered the human heart, what God has prepared for those who love him" (1 Cor. 2:9). Enter even into the human mind, rather. So, the revelation comes to us in the form of stories—myths. Stories that express deep truths. It comes to us in metaphor. And it comes to us in poetry. The reason we constantly sing and pray the poems of the Scriptures—the Psalms, the canticles, and so on—is because there is a richness there.

We need to listen to the Psalms as poetry to really get what they are trying to convey to us. The genius of Hebrew poetry was not in rhyme or rhythm, although there is some of that. But not much. It's mainly in the richness and the metaphors. But, precisely, the Hebrew poetry put metaphor upon metaphor upon metaphor saying the same thing but using different words which had a different richness, a different nuance. That's what Psalm 119 does to strophe after strophe.

You are just, O LORD, and your ordinance is right. / You have pronounced your decrees in justice and a perfect faithfulness. / My zeal consumes me because my foes forget your words. / Your promise is very sure and your servant loves it. / I am mean and contemptible, but your precepts I have not forgotten. / Your justice is everlasting justice, and your law is permanent. / Though stress and anguish have come to me, your commands are my delight. / Your decrees are forever just; give me discernment that I may live. / I call out with all my heart; answer me, O LORD; I will observe your statutes (Psalm 118 [119]:129–145).[16]

We find here the poet using the words *ordinance*, *decrees*, *word*, *promise*, *law*, *precept*, *command*, *statutes*. All these words are trying to bring out something of the richness of what it is that God has given us in revelation. He has given us his word, his message. If you listen to each of those words, each has a different nuance for us.

When you hear of "ordinance," what are you thinking? Something that is established by someone in authority. When you hear of a "decree"—that's someone who is up at the top. "The decree of Caesar Augustus went forth and the whole world moved." Where it speaks of "your word"—vitally, intimately present. "Your promise"—you have commitment, something that is going to open out and unfold. "Your precept"—kind of personal, authoritative but personal. "Your law"—that's rather impersonal. It's something kind of laid down for everybody. "Your command"—that's the top sergeant: "Attention!" "Go to it!" "Your statutes"—something a little less important than law but a little more amenable.

Above All, Listen

Of all those, Benedict chose "precept."[17] Precept has a certain authority, definitely. It has something very personal about it. It isn't something abstract like law. It's much more personal. In his Rule, Benedict is speaking in a personal way. In fact, he goes on to say, "incline the ear of your heart."[18] The "your" he uses there is not *cordis vestri* but *cordis tui*. He is talking to the very intimate, *singular* person.

Benedict calls us: "Listen, son. . . ." Listen to what? ". . . to the precepts." To the personal but authoritative word of the *magistri*, of the master, who is not just the authority but as an authority who has a fullness of wisdom and a role to teach. His words—his precept—is something that is not just an ordinance—do it this way or that way—it's a call to wisdom. It's the wise leading, and the wise directing. So he's calling us to that—"to listen," knowing that here we are going to find the wisdom of life. This wisdom is brought to us with a certain authority because it is of the Lord, of the Master.

Certainly this is what our fathers of Molesme who went to Cîteaux, the men of York who went to Fountains, and the founders of Gethsemani who came here to Conyers possessed—a zeal and desire to hear and live by the wisdom of Saint Benedict and the wisdom of the Rule which is an expression of a Gospel life. Their desire was of a way of living the Gospel that brings a deep union with the Lord Jesus who is the true Master. This union is found in a union of will, mind, and heart—of oneness. *I always do what is pleasing to him* (Jn. 8:29). And we can say, "I always seek to do the things that please the Lord." So I listen to the precepts of my Master, Jesus. This is the attitude that Benedict invites us to bring as we listen to the Holy Rule as an expression of the holy Gospels.

MAY THE DIVINE ASSISTANCE
REMAIN WITH US ALWAYS AMEN

III ❧ FREELY RECEIVE AND EFFECTIVELY FULFILL

¹Listen carefully, my son, to the master's instructions, and attend to them with the ear of your heart. This is advice from a father who loves you; welcome it, and faithfully put it into practice. ²The labor of obedience will bring you back to him from whom you had drifted through the sloth of disobedience. ³This message of mine is for you, then, if you are ready to give up your own will, once and for all, and armed with the strong and noble weapons of obedience to do battle for the true King, Christ the Lord.

—Prologue
THE RULE OF SAINT BENEDICT

The whole of the Rule is summed up in those first two words: *Obsculta, o fili.* "Listen, son." If we can do that—really listen as the son—the wonder of it! We have been baptized into Christ. We are the beloved sons of God. And just to sit with that reality! There is a part of us that immediately squirms. "Me? This poor, weak, stupid sinner?" "Me? The beloved son of God?" Yes! Yes, you are the beloved son of God.

And how does the son listen? The son listens with such total openness that the Father is able to pour forth his whole being into the son. The son receives the fullness of that and returns it to the Father in that mutual love who is Holy Spirit. A complete gift, divine.

This is what we celebrate this week [Pentecost]—preparing for, longing for that outpouring of the Father. He pours out his whole being, his Holy Spirit, upon us, his sons, so that we can return to him something that is really worthy of him. For we do not know how to pray as we ought, but the Spirit prays in us (Rom. 8:26). Wide open. Receive all from the Father, so we can give all to the Father and truly be sons who receive the spirit of adoption and cry out, "*Abba*, Father!" (Rom. 8:15). It is all right there in the first two words of the Rule: Listen, son.

INCLINE THE EAR OF YOUR HEART

Et inclina aurem cordis tui. "Incline the ear of your heart."[19] Listen to what? *Et admonitionem pii patris libenter excipe et efficaciter comple.* "Freely receive and effectively fulfill the admonition of your loving father." If we could really have this spiritual insight to see that everything that is asked of us, whether it is asked of us through the Scriptures, through the Church, through obedience to the superior or to the brethren, through the experiences of life—whether it be sickness, health, etcetera—is really *admonitionem pii patris*, "the word of your loving father." As Saint Paul says, "For those who love God, all things work together for good" (cf. Rom. 8:28).

It is beautiful Latin: *libenter excipe et efficaciter comple.* "Freely receive and effectively carry out." It immediately brings to mind that story in the Gospel of the two sons (Mt. 21:29–31). The first one says, "Oh yes! Yes, Father! I'll go." The other one says, "Oh, no! No, Father! I can't go! I'm too busy." But the one who says *yes* does not go, and the one who says *no*, goes. Which are we?

Sometimes it is very difficult to freely receive. The Lord certainly understands that. He sweat blood in Gethsemani before he could finally say *yes*. He understood the son who said *no* but then went. Sometimes it is hard to be a wholehearted *yes* to what God is asking of us. The fullness comes when we can do that—when we can freely hear and we can effectively carry out what God asks of us. That is what we are striving for.

Benedict goes on: "So that we might return to him through the labor of obedience from whom we have departed by the laziness of disobedience."[20] Again, a beautiful balance in Latin. *Per oboedientiae laborem redeas, a quo per inoboedientiae desidiam recesseras.* "That we return to him by the labor of obedience from whom we have departed by the sloth of disobedience."

The biblical image is there, of course, of the Prodigal Son who went to a faraway place (Lk. 15:11–32). He went away from the father and then he returned. We all have departed in sin, and we all are returning. It is interesting, though: He speaks about *per inoboedientiae desidiam*. Through the "sloth of disobedience" we have departed from him.

Benedict was an old man when he was writing this, and I think we know more and more as we get older what the sloth of disobedience is. When we are young, we are energetic. We can do it all. As the years go by, and we get old, we get tired, we get sick, and so on. It is very tempting to use those as excuses and not keep all there with the Lord. It is easy to fall into this sloth of disobedience and let things go. It gets harder to get things done.

I am embarrassed by the fact that I still have not finished unpacking not from the last trip but the trip before that! It is taking so long to get things unpacked. There was a time when I would come from a trip and within two hours I would be unpacked and everything in its place. But it now takes a lot more push to get even ordinary things done.

Yet, the Lord asks us to be wholehearted in our obedience, whatever that is. To be all there. So it is a labor. He speaks of the labor of obedience. Yes, it is a job to obey, to keep at it right to the end.

CHOOSING FREELY

That word *oboedientiae* is a wonderful word. English does not quite capture it easily. Freedom is a part of it, like liberation. *Libenter* comes from the deep depths of our own being. It is *our* decision. But it carries with it the connotation of joy, as well. When you do something wholeheartedly—when it really expresses you—that is *libenter*.

At the ordination rite in the old days, the bishop would call forth the people and ask them if they wanted to go ahead. They would say, "*Libenter*." "I choose freely, and I want to. I want to!" Benedict says, *libenter excipe*. This is the same idea that he is trying to bring out in chapter fifty-eight. He speaks of the qualities that we are supposed to be looking for in somebody who truly seeks God. He has zeal for the work of God, zeal for obedience, and zeal for the humble way of monastic life. *Libenter* is that; it is a fullness of being there. *Libenter excipe*. "Joyfully receive!"

We can avoid hearing the word of God. We do not read the notes on the community bulletin board. We keep our distance from the superior. We walk around with a blindfold on. Things like this. But *libenter excipe*—we are wide open. What do you want, Lord? Speak, Lord, your servant wants to hear (1 Sam. 3:9). This is the attitude for *lectio* [spiritual reading]. *Lectio* is the place where we very personally come to the Lord and say, "I'm here and want to hear."

I really enjoy *lectio*. I think it is just this. I go there each day and say, "What do you have to say to me now? What do you want now? What's the meaning of this?" That is, I think, *libenter excipe*. There is a longing.

Why? Ultimately, why?

Because we want to be united with God, and God is where his will is. It is a union of wills. It is because this is where Christ is. Christ is *libenter excipe*. "Freely receiving." Wide open to the Father. This is where the joy of the life comes. It is hard for us, in a way, to be that wholeheartedness.

BEING *YES* TO THE LORD

We have all been brainwashed to varying degrees by this world and by the advertising in this world—the media of a consumer society. It is sad to think of how many millions of dollars and how much some of the finest minds are employed to convince people that they need this, that, and the other thing.

While I was sitting in the hospital [recently], the television was of course blaring in the room.[21] I was tempted to get out my watch and start timing it. I suspect that about 25 percent, at least, of the time is advertisements. They are using all sorts of brilliant ideas and arts to convince people, "You can't be happy without this." Whether it is a car, a shampoo, or whatever it is. Even we older ones who didn't have television went through it in other ways. The media advertisement has always been there but never as strong as in our current times. The consuming society is pounding into us that you cannot be happy without this, that, and the other thing. While we try to leave that behind, there is a lot of it that is still in our thinking. It could be something like, "If I don't get so much sleep." Or, "If I don't get so many vitamins." If I don't get this, that, and the other thing. These things come in and prevent us from just simply being able to say *yes* to the Lord.

Sure, I take care of my health and try to live a balanced life. I use my mind and I keep my body in good shape. But the bottom line: Yes, Lord! When we can be that—a complete yes, *libenter excipe*—we freely accept whatever God disposes for us. Then, we are, indeed, filled with joy. We just go forward and do it. We do it as fully and as well as we can with the Lord, and we accept our limitations, too. We have our limitations, and we have to accept them. Yet, there is still a profound joy, because the deepest disposition in our soul and being is *yes! Libenter excipe.*

RECEIVE THE HOLY SPIRIT

This fits in well with where we are right now in the life of the Christian Church and for us monks especially. This is the Abbey of Our Lady of the Holy Spirit. This is the abbey of the spouse of the Spirit. There is nothing Mary wants to give us more than the Spirit. Pentecost Sunday is the great feast of the outpouring of the Spirit. If we could be wide open; if we can say with our whole being, *libenter*—joyfully, freely, wholeheartedly I open myself to receive the Spirit in all the fullness that God wants to give the Spirit to me—then this will be a tremendous Pentecost for us all.

In the last couple days of this profound retreat—the Church gathered around Mary in prayer—let us pray deeply for the whole Church because we are in the Body of Christ. Especially let us pray for our community, this community of Holy Spirit. That it be a time of wonderful outpouring of the joy and the love and the empowerment that belongs to us as the sons who receive Holy Spirit from the Father.

MAY THE DIVINE ASSISTANCE REMAIN WITH US ALWAYS AMEN

IV ❧ TURNING TO JESUS CHRIST

¹Listen carefully, my son, to the master's instructions, and attend to them with the ear of your heart. This is advice from a father who loves you; welcome it, and faithfully put it into practice. ²The labor of obedience will bring you back to him from whom you had drifted through the sloth of disobedience. ³This message of mine is for you, then, if you are ready to give up your own will, once and for all, and armed with the strong and noble weapons of obedience to do battle for the true King, Christ the Lord.

—Prologue
THE RULE OF SAINT BENEDICT

Let us return to the Holy Rule. I think we can move on to the second sentence, now! As I sit with the Rule, I realize more and more why Saint Benedict said, "Let this Rule be read frequently in community."[22] The Rule is so much like the Scriptures—it is so full of Scriptures—that every time you read the Rule, you get new or deeper insights and appreciation.

This second sentence is important. In this sentence Benedict tells us for whom he is writing. Conversely, he is telling us who has a call, a vocation, to live according to his Rule. He makes a very fundamental statement. Just like the first sentence—*Obsculta, o fili*, "listen, my son"[23]—it is a personal, immediate, and intimate expression. *Ad te ergo nunc mihi sermo dirigitur.*[24] To you. He uses *te*, the singular and intimate. He is talking directly to you and me. *Ad te*, "to you."

Ergo nunc, "now." Right here and now. The immediacy of it. It is in this moment we live. My first spiritual father would say, "The past and the future are other forms of self. God is now." God is the eternal now. In the past, we are off in our memories. In the future, we are off in our imagination. The reality in life is in the now. You find this in all of the spiritual traditions. What is being sought in the different methods of meditation is to be present here, now. Benedict says, "To you, now, I'm speaking." *Mihi sermo.*

In the Eastern Byzantine tradition, when someone is thinking of becoming a monk, he visits monasteries until he finds a spiritual father in whom he feels he can entrust himself. Then he says to him, "Father, give me a word of life." Give me a word. Benedict is saying here, *Ad te ergo nunc mihi sermo dirigitur.* "To you do I direct my word now." He is expressing his willingness to be our spiritual father. But who is he talking to? He goes on to make that clear.

THE MEANING OF CONVERSION

Quisquis abrenuntians propriis voluntatibus, Domino Christo vero regi militaturus, oboedientiae fortissima atque praeclara arma sumis. "If you are ready to give up your own will, and armed with the strong and noble weapons of obedience to do battle for the true King, Christ the Lord." *Quisquis* is a wide-open word meaning something like "whoever." Benedict wrote his Rule for the rich and the poor, to the learned and the unlearned, to the slave and the free. This has been true of Cistercian monasteries from the very beginning. Cistercian monasticism not only accepted men who were serfs and unlettered but gave them full equality in the community of the solemnly professed. Our communities are open to men of all kinds—learned and unlearned, young and old.

Abrenuntians propriis voluntatibus, Domino Christo. One is "turning from his own will and turning to Christ." This is conversion. The Latin has it as "whoever wants to convert." The word conversion is *conversio*—to turn to be with. *Con. Versio.* It is not so much turning away from, but what are you turning to. You have to turn away in order to turn to. If I turn over here to speak to Brother William, I am turning my back to poor Father Richard here. My concern is that I want to talk to William. So when we turn to one, we have to leave the other.

That is something to be aware of. I have had more than a couple times a brother tell me that he thought such-and-such a brother did not care for him, or was ignoring him. In each case, it was not that at all. The other brother was concerned with someone else. It was *not* that he was not thinking of this brother. Maybe we should all have the sensitivity to realize that every time we turn to someone, we are turning away from someone else. What if I turn to talk to Brother William, and Father Richard starts to say, "Oh, the abbot doesn't like me anymore. He turns his back on me"? It is not that at all. We need to be sensitive, but at the same time we need to be realistic about our relations in the community.

FRIENDSHIP IN A COMMUNITY

In the late 1960s, seminaries and religious theologates were moving from the country into the cities, perhaps wisely so. Their almost monastic life was not necessarily a good preparation for a diocesan priest or for an active religious. The Jesuits of the Midwestern province had a big theologate at St. Marys, Kansas, which is way out in the wheat fields. They decided to move the theologate into St. Louis and bought a big hotel on Lindell Boulevard, across the street from St. Louis University. They had to remodel the hotel to suit a Jesuit community, and so they asked Dr. Menninger, head of the Menninger Behavioral Institute in Kansas, to advise them on how they should reshape this hotel to best support community life. Menninger wrote an extensive report of seventy-five pages. For a man to function well, Menninger wrote, he needs a solid, grounding relationship with a stable community. Then he needs an acquaintance group, eight or ten or twelve people that he is comfortable with, to talk with and be with. Then he needs one or two real friends.

We have a stable community here at this Abbey of Our Lady of the Holy Spirit. We are a community solidly established by solemn vows.[25] We really have a sense of belonging to this community. Traditionally, our monks have been identified by the community to which they belong: Bernard of Clairvaux (1090–1153), Aelred of Rievaulx (1109–1167). We do the same today. I am Basil of Conyers and so on. We belong to this community.

The acquaintance of friends develops among the men in the novitiate or juniorate or those with whom you work. I have seen that especially at Spencer Abbey, where the monks working at Trappist Preserves are one group, while the monks working in the Holy Rood Guild, infirmary, or kitchen form other groups of friends. We get friends around the community with whom we are comfortable. Perhaps it is through working with them or just being with them. Then we have one or two special friends. It is probably limited to one or two because we do not have the time or psychological-emotional energy to develop a deep friendship with more than one or two people at a time.

We have to realize the value of people having a special friend in the community—somebody they can share more fully with and be supported with. Yet, as one develops a special friendship with somebody and gives time to that person, others may feel neglected. Friends have to be aware that their friendship can never be exclusive. It is open to the whole community. In spending more time with somebody, he is not turning his back on the rest of the community. You should never do that. He is necessarily spending more time, however, with the brother with whom he is trying to develop a closer and deeper relationship.

DISCERNING WITH THE WILL

Benedict speaks about what he turns away from and what he turns to. The turning away is not the important thing. *Conversio* is turning to, to be with. He does say, *abrenuntians propriis voluntatibus*. "Renounces one's own will or self-will." He uses a strong word: *abrenuntians*. The monk not just renounces. Benedict adds to it the word *ab*, the monk goes away from. What is he going away from? *Propriis voluntatibus*. "His own proper will." Our Cistercian fathers developed this a great deal: the difference between what they call the *voluntas propria* and *voluntas communis*.[26] The proper will (self-will, one's own will) and the common will. What do they mean by the common will?

The most important thing—the thing that makes us men, separates us from the rest of the animal kingdom— is that we are rational animals. We have a mind and a will. We have an intellect that guides the will. The will is the essential part of a man. Man has a will, but we have been baptized into Christ. We have become one with Christ, and the Holy Spirit has been poured into our hearts so that we can cry, "*Abba*, Father!" (Rom. 8:15). Christ's spirit—Christ's will, in a sense—has been given to us. Christ's total being in love has been given to us.

The *voluntas communis* is, in fact, when we become fully integrated; our human will is one with the divine will—with the will of Christ. It is a common will because everyone who is a member of Christ comes together in that one will. So we want complete integration with Christ. Benedict says, "giving up your own will"— renouncing your own will to be one with Christ. The way he expresses it brings it out.

THE BEAUTY OF OBEDIENCE

Domino Christo vero regi militaturus, oboedientiae fortissima atque praeclara arma sumis. "Armed with the strong and noble weapons of obedience to do battle for the true King, Christ the Lord." We may not care much for Benedict's military imagery, but remember who he was—a man of his own time. The military imagery speaks of dedication, discipline, fidelity, and certainly obedience. The monk is one who takes on the strong and brilliant armor of obedience to fight under Christ the true King, Christ our Lord[27]—to give ourselves totally over to being a follower, a supporter, to be one with Christ. It is by taking on the armor of obedience.

Benedict uses a military term: *fortissima atque praeclara.* *Fortissima* is a superlative—the strongest, most powerful, and brilliant armor of obedience. For Benedict, there is a no more powerful shield, or protection for us, than obedience. It is beautiful. *Praeclara.* It is like the light of day, most wonderful. Why? Because it is the way of Christ. He came not to do his own will but to do the will of his Father (Lk. 22:42). He sought always to do the things that please the Father (Jn. 8:29). He was obedient unto death even death on a cross (Phil. 2:8). Where does obedience lead? In its fullness, obedience leads us to complete mystical union with God. To be completely one with Christ to the Father and the Holy Spirit. That is what it is all about.

But obedience is lived in the everyday sort of things: getting up when the bell rings, going to choir, doing our work, and other things we are asked to do. As Benedict says, the monastery is the school of the Lord's service. We have to learn about obedience. We may immediately choose to renounce the world and to follow Christ, but to live that totally day by day is something we have to learn. For years, we have been doing our own will. Before you came to the monastery, whose will did you do all of the time? We did our own will. Me, too. In the monastery, we are to learn how to completely renounce our self-will.

The self-will is very subtle, always trying to get into the act. The self-will gets us to do what *we* want. It could be good things, too. This is why the conversion is not adequate if we are just turning away from something. In turning away from the world and coming to the monastery, it leaves an enormous void. What is that void going to be filled with? Self-will. Good things, sure. Taking care of my health, being sure I eat properly, exercise, enjoying nature, enjoying music, enjoying different things, getting projects going, studying—we can do all these things, yet they could be self-willed and not lead us to unity with God at all. So, what do we turn to? That is important. We turn to be totally with Christ. That is why Benedict will say, "Prefer absolutely nothing to the love of Christ."[28]

That's the whole meaning of obedience, renunciation, and conversion: to be one with Christ—to come to the fullness of who we are as men who have been divinized, made partakers of the divine nature and life, raised up to be Christ-people. We are to be one with Christ in the common will to the Father and the Holy Spirit. Benedict brings this out in the third verse: to want that one will with Christ.

FOUR DEGREES OF LOVE

Our father Saint Bernard said there are four degrees of love.[29] The first degree was to love ourselves—to appreciate and really celebrate who we are. We are one of God's greatest creations; we have been Christ-ed. In the second degree, we begin to really love God for what he has done for us. Because of that experience, in the third degree we come to love God because he is so good. The fourth degree, says Bernard, is rarely fully attained in this life; it is when we come to love ourselves for the sake of God. We have turned from our own will in order to turn completely to the will of Christ. The will of Christ is that we be loved immensely, be cared for, come to all fullness. When our love for Christ has been so strong that we really love ourselves for Christ's sake, then we have it all put together in Christ, for Christ, through Christ, by Christ.

The Holy Rule is for men who want to get out of the trap of self-will and really come to complete union and communion with Christ in love.

MAY THE DIVINE ASSISTANCE [AMEN]
REMAIN WITH US ALWAYS

V ❧ EVERYTHING BEGINS WITH GOD

⁴First of all, every time you begin a good work, you must pray to him most earnestly to bring it to perfection. ⁵In his goodness, he has already counted us as his sons, and therefore we should never grieve him by our evil actions. ⁶With his good gifts which are in us, we must obey him at all times that he may never become the angry father who disinherits his sons, ⁷nor the dread lord, enraged by our sins, who punishes us forever as worthless servants for refusing to follow him to glory.

—Prologue

THE RULE OF SAINT BENEDICT

Having celebrated the solemnity of Saint Benedict, I think it is time to get back to the Holy Rule. I used to wonder why Saint Bernard, who started commenting on the Song of Songs in 1136, had only gotten halfway through the second chapter when he died in 1153. Now, I am beginning to see why that is the case. I have been here almost a year, and we are up to almost the fourth verse of the prologue.

In the first paragraph of the prologue, Benedict has called us to listen, listen as sons who want to return. The story of the Prodigal Son is perhaps one of the central stories of the Gospels (Lk. 15:11–32). It so expresses God's tremendous love for us. No matter what we do, how much we squander all that he has given us, he is longing for us to come back to him. The most striking thing in that story is the young son when he arrives. He has his plan worked out, including how he is going to do something to justify himself, to earn some little place in his father's affection. He has this plan all worked out; he has prepared it. We find in the story, our Lord says twice, he repeats it, the son is going to tell his father, "Father, I am not worthy to be your son. I will work as a servant." He has this plan of how he is going to do it. At that moment of encounter with the father, he lets his plan go, and he is wide open to let the father just pour out upon him his prodigal love and give him everything—new clothes, new shoes, celebration—everything. Just poured out. This is what the Father wants. He wants us to forget what is behind. All right, we have all been a bunch of stupid sinners. Leave it all behind and just let the Father pour out his divine love upon us. That is what God wants: He wants to lavish his love upon us.

This is Benedict's whole thing: "Listen, son. Listen. Return to your Father whom you have separated from by the sloth of our disobedience. Let us return to him by the way of obedience—the way of union and communion."

EVERYTHING BEGINS WITH GOD

Benedict speaks to us: "Now listen, son. Do you want to return by obedience? You want to return to communion and union with the Father?" He begins the second paragraph [verse four of the prologue] *In primis*, "in the first place"—this is the first thing you have to do. And what is that? What is the first thing we have to do according to Saint Benedict? He says, *In primis, ut quicquid agendum inchaos bonum, ab eo peffici instantissima oratione deposcas.*[30] "The first thing you have to do is pray with most insistent prayer."

Instantissima. "Insistent and persistent." He uses a powerful superlative. We pray with the most insistent prayer that he will bring it to true perfection—*perfacio*, the same word as perfection. *Perfacio*—to make it full, to bring it to its full realization. That he will do what we have begun, what we seek to do.

He continues, *quicquid agendum inchoas bonum.* "Whatever good—*whatever good*—you want to do," you begin to pray, first of all, with most insistent prayer, that he will bring it to perfection.

This is what Benedict is trying to bring out in his steps of humility—everything begins with God. Jesus said it very simply: "Without me you can do nothing" (Jn. 15:5). We all bow our heads yes, and we all have our plans. Like that son coming home, we say, Well, I am going to do this. I am going to serve as a good servant and earn some little corner. We have to let all of our own plans go. Nothing comes from us. Everything comes from him. The will to pray even comes from him. It all comes from him. So we pray *instantissima oratione,* "with most urgent prayer," that he will carry it through.

And then it is interesting the reason that Benedict brings for this. Why do we pray that we will come to the fullness of all that we are called for? *Perfacio* means *per,* "through," *facio,* "make." This whole thing is "made through" to the fullness that it is called to.

Why should we seek perfection? *Ut qui nos iam filiorum dignatus est numero computare non debet aliquando de malis actibus nostris contristari.*[31] "In his goodness, he has already counted us as his sons, and therefore we should never grieve him by our evil actions." Because God has been *so good* that he has called us to be his very own sons, who has adopted us, has raised us up to be sharers of the divine nature in life. We want to do this so as not to cause a disappointment, not to cause sorrow to this all-good Father. This wonderful Father! This is why we want to be perfect. So we do not disappoint him who is so good—so good to us. He has deigned to make us his sons. If we could only grasp this: God has taken you and me, who have been called forth into being out of nothing by his great love, and made us his very sons, sharers of the divine nature of life. We do not want to cause sorrow or disappoint him.

THE FATHER HAS ADOPTED YOU

All of the classical fairy tales popularize biblical evangelical values. One theme that comes again and again is the adoption. The poor little beggar is adopted by the king and made the prince. Cinderella is taken out of the ashes and made the great princess. Again and again, the story of wonderment, because this is what our hearts long for. This is what we know we are called to, this fullness.

Perhaps you have read or seen the play or movie of that wonderful story by Victor Hugo (1802–1885), *Les Misérables* (1862). The hero is Jean Valjean. Because of the experience he has of the archbishop as the prodigal father, who reaches out to Jean in the very moment that Jean is stealing stuff from him, Jean himself becomes the merciful father of an adopted little girl, the child of the prostitute who died and he promised to take care of. He risks his life again and again for that child. His whole happiness is the happiness of that child. It is a beautiful evangelical story. God so loves us. This wonderful Father who has adopted you and made you his very beloved son.

Benedict turns to the other side and paints the picture. He says, *Ita enim ei omni tempore de bonis suis in nobis parendum est ut non solum iratus pater.* "All the time," *omni tempore.*[32] Always, we want to obey him using the very goods that he gives us. *De bonis suis.* We want to use all that he has given us in complete harmony with his will so that it comes to the fullness that he wants it to come to. Our plans and ideas are always going to fall short. He makes a contrast here several times. *A malis nostris.*[33] *De bonis suis.*[34] "Our evil" and "his good," and our evil is just a lack of good. The good is absent because the good does not come from us. It comes from him. Anything that comes from us is evil because it is lacking in some of the good that it could have. The whole thing is *his way.* All the time, we want to obey him, to be in harmony with him and his holy will, using the good he has given us, using the grace, the gifts, the talents he has given us. But *his way,* so that they can come to the fullness that *he wants.*

Then Benedict goes to the other side. He says, "So that not only as an angry father he will not have to disinherit us, but also as an angry lord he will not, because of our evil deeds as most wicked servants, he will hand us over to eternal punishment."[35] He uses a superlative, *nequissimos,* "the most evil servants."

THE WAY TO GLORY

Qui enum sequi noluerint ad gloriam is the final thing he says.[36] In good Latin grammar, you always put the important thing at the end—the message you want to give. We want to obey him and use all of our gifts to the fullness so that he will not have to disinherit us. He will not, as an angry Lord, have to punish us because *qui eum sequi noluerint ad gloriam*—"because we have refused to follow him to glory." It is our choice. We can obey him using the gifts and come to the fullness he wants, or we can refuse. *Noluerint sequi.* "Refuse to follow him." Refuse to walk in his way, the way that leads to glory.

Now obviously, none of us would ever choose *not* to follow the Lord to glory, but it is because we do not see that this is the way. Our pride leads us to think another way is the way. This is why *lectio* is so fundamental to our lives. In *lectio* we are constantly asking: "Lord, speak. Help me to see. Help me to see what is the way to glory. What is the way to be who I am called to be as your beloved son? What is the way I can live in the fullness of who I am? How can I know who I really am?"

It is little by little that we begin to understand who we are as men who have been baptized into Christ and raised up to be made sharers of the divine nature as beloved sons of God and see that his way is the way. We are brought more and more into that mystery—the things that human reason cannot see, human understanding cannot see. Human understanding and reason plan that *this* is the better way of doing it, *that* is the better way of doing it. Those things do not work. They are not brought under the divine plan which is for each of us to come to the fullness of divine glory.

These first two paragraphs are woven together. It is the son who has decided to say *yes* and to come back to the Father, to follow the Father's way to glory. It is a choice we make—*yes*. This is why Benedict emphasizes humility. Humility is truth. It is accepting the reality of "from me nothing comes but sin." I cannot do it. All good comes from him. As he says at the beginning of chapter five, the first degree of humility is obedience—accepting that God's way is the way.[37]

AND OUR HAPPINESS

The prologue leads up to the next to last verse. "But as we progress in this way of life and in faith, we shall run on the path of God's commandments, our hearts overflowing with the inexpressible delight of love."[38] Happiness lies in knowing what we want and then knowing we have it or are on the way of getting it. Benedict is saying: the way to what we really want is what God wants. The way to it is the way of obedience, the path of God's commandments. We are filled with joy as we run along this path because we know it is leading to the fulfillment of everything we can possibly want and even more.

At the end of the ladder of humility, after the twelfth step, Benedict says, "Now, therefore, after ascending all these steps of humility, the monk will quickly arrive at that *perfect love* of God which *casts out fear*" (1 Jn. 4:18).[39] We know and live in the fullness of that knowledge and love.

This conversion is what our life is about. It is the turning toward the truth that God so loves us and wants our absolute and complete happiness. The way to that is, "Yes, Lord! Yes, Lord!" Doing it God's way instead of my way. A complete *yes* to the Lord which Mary modeled at the beginning. "Be it done unto me according to your word" (cf. Lk. 1:38). We repeat that word in our *lectio*, in our liturgy, in our sharing—to hear God's word, God's plan, God's promise. May we all come to that immense joy. The joy right now! Benedict is not saying that this is something that comes in heaven. It is something that we are to come to even in this life—an inexpressible joy because we are running in the way of God's commands. We know this is leading to all fullness. That is where our joy lies—the experience, knowledge, and hope of a tremendous love. How much we are loved! The Lord is willing to show us the way through the Church, through the order, through the community, through *lectio*, through obedience—the way to fullness of joy and happiness.

Not having experienced such a total self-giving love, it is hard for us to believe in that. That is why we have to go again and again to the Gospels to hear the stories by which Jesus teaches and see in his actions by which he speaks of how much we are loved. How the only desire God has of the whole of his creation project, as immense and wondrous as it is, is your happiness and my happiness. That is what it is all about, because that is how good and how loving our God is and how important we are to him.

MAY THE DIVINE ASSISTANCE AMEN
REMAIN WITH US ALWAYS

VI ❖ NOW IS THE TIME
TO LET GOD SPEAK TO YOU

⁸Let us get up then, at long last, for the Scriptures rouse us when they say: It is high time for us to arise from sleep *(Rom. 13:11).* *⁹Let us open our eyes to the light that comes from God, and our ears to the voice from heaven that every day calls out this charge:* ¹⁰If you hear his voice today, do not harden your hearts *(Ps. 95:8).* *¹¹And again:* You that have ears to hear, listen to what the Spirit says to the churches *(Rev. 2:7).* *¹²And what does he say?* Come and listen to me, sons; I will teach you the fear of the Lord *(Ps. 34:12).* ¹³Run while you have the light *of life,* that the darkness *of death* may not overtake you *(Jn. 12:35).* *¹⁴Seeking his workman in a multitude of people, the Lord calls out to him and lifts his voice again:* ¹⁵Is there anyone here who yearns for life and desires to see good days? *(Ps. 34:13).* *¹⁶If you hear this and your answer is "I do," God then directs these words to you:* ¹⁷If you desire true and eternal life, keep your tongue free from vicious talk and your lips from all deceit; turn away from evil and do good; let peace be your quest and aim *(Ps. 34:14–15).* *¹⁸Once you have done this, my* eyes will be upon *you* and *my* ears will listen for your prayers; and even before you ask me, I will say *to you: Here I am (Isa. 58:9). ¹⁹What, dear brothers, is more delightful than this voice of the Lord calling to us? ²⁰See how the Lord in his love shows us the way of life. ²¹Clothed then with faith and the performance of good works, let us set out on this way, with the Gospel for our guide, that we may deserve to see him* who has called us to his kingdom *(1 Thess. 2:12).*

—Prologue
THE RULE OF SAINT BENEDICT

We have been walking gently through the prologue of the Holy Rule. Benedict speaks to us as his sons—prodigal sons—who once departed from the Father by what he calls our "sloth of disobedience." He wants us to return to him by the "labor of obedience."[40] He went on to say, "The first thing you have to do is pray that God, who has begun this good work in you—has given you the will to want to return to the Father—will bring this through."[41] That *he* will bring it through. We cannot do it ourselves; we depend on him.

Benedict goes on and talks about this way. The prologue in this new section has two sections. We begin at verse 8, which goes to verse 21, and then from 22 to 39.[42] The second part is, in a sense, a repetition of the first part, but it emphasizes two things very dear to Benedict: humility and responsiveness. The whole is tied together in the beginning of the section when he speaks about "now is the time."[43] At the end of the second section, in verse 38, he speaks about why God gives us this "now."[44] Remember, when Benedict was writing this—it was the last thing he wrote—he was a very old man. He is talking about longevity. He is asking, Why has the Lord kept me going all this time?

Having told us to pray, Benedict continues:

Let us get up then, at long last, for the Scriptures rouse us when they say: *It is high time for us to arise from sleep* (Rom. 13:11). Let us open our eyes to the light that comes from God, and our ears to the voice from heaven that every day calls out this charge: *If you hear his voice today, do not harden your hearts* (Ps. 95:8).[45]

Benedict is saying, "*Now* is the time. No matter how old you are or where you are on the journey, now is the time to open your eyes and to open your ears and let God in to speak to you." *Hora est iam*.[46] Now is "the time to rise from sleep." *Et apertis oculis nostris*.[47] Opening our eyes to the *deificum lumen*.[48] That word can be translated either passively or actively. The author here translates it passively—"the light which comes from God." I think it is more properly translated "the deifying light," the light that makes us to become like unto God—grace. The divine light. The deifying light. Open your eyes to the deifying light.

Then, *attonitis auribus audiamus divina vox.*[49] "Tune your ears to hear the divine voice." The translation says, "the voice from heaven," but the Latin is "the divine voice." This is how Benedict looked to the Scriptures, especially the psalm that he is talking about here—Psalm 95. He quotes the psalm. Tune your ears to really hear God talking to you through the Scriptures, through the Psalms, and so on. Wake up!

We all tend to a certain somnolence at the Office, at our *lectio.* And if our life is not filled with as much joy, excitement, and meaningfulness as we want it to be (and as it should be), it is because we are somnolent. We are not wide awake and listening, letting in the divine light, the divine word that comes to us through the Scriptures, in the Office, and in our private *lectio.*

Benedict is saying, Let us get up now. Let us really listen. Let us see what God is saying to us here. He says, *audiamus cotidie clamans.*[50] "Every day he is crying to us." Actually, the psalm he quotes here, as the older monks know, is the psalm we began with every day— Psalm 95. *Hodie si vocem eius audieritis, nolite obdurare corda vestra.*[51] "Today if you hear his voice, do not harden your hearts." The invitatory at vigils every day was this psalm. Benedict chose it precisely for that—to make us wake up and say, "Today. Now. Here is the time to listen." No matter what has gone before, now is the time to listen, to open all the promise that is ahead for us.

Of course, Psalm 95 refers to the Exodus. *Hodie si vocem eius audieritis, nolite obdurare corda vestra.* "If you hear his voice today, do not harden your hearts" (v. 8). It is a time when Pharaoh hardened his heart and would not allow the people to go into the desert. We have gone into the desert. We have heard the Lord's call and have gone into the desert, but there is always a danger that our hearts remain hardened, that our hearts will still stay settled in the things of the world. The whole labor of our life is to come to that purity of heart when, finally, we have been able to expel from our hearts all the worldliness, all the attraction that things of the world still hold for us—to do things, to have things, the ambitions, all of these sort of things that enslave us—the things that enslave the people in the bondage of sin, which is typified by the bondage of the holy people in Israel.

Don't harden your hearts. Let your hearts be wide open, subtle, ready to be moved, be shaped, to be formed by the divine light, by the divine word. Benedict is calling us to "*Hodie.*"[52] Today. Right now is the time of new opportunity.

New grace. New openness. New excitement in the divine love.

Again, he says, *You that have ears to hear, hear what the Spirit says to the churches* (cf. Rev. 2:7).[53]

What does the Spirit say? *Come and listen to me, sons; I will teach you the fear of the Lord* (cf. Ps. 34:12).[54] *"Run while you have the light* of life, *that the darkness* of death *may not overtake you"* (cf. Jn. 12:35).[55] God is still giving us life, so that today we can make a whole new beginning no matter where we are on the journey or how long we have been on the journey; today we begin.

THE IMPORTANCE OF HEARING

In this short paragraph, it is striking how many times Benedict uses the word related with hearing. He has *auribus, audiamus, audiat, audiendi, audite, aures, audieritis*—seven times in a matter of five sentences or so. As we have seen, it is the key word of the whole Rule—*obsculta, o fili.*[56] Listen, hear, hearing. Benedict is convinced: if we really hear the word of God we cannot but be a complete *yes* to it. It is a word of tremendous love, power, and presence. This is why he places *lectio* and the *Opus Dei* as so fundamental. That is where we hear God. We hear God in the divine light. If we allow that divine light to shine upon us through that word, it would be transforming.

Back in the 1950s, quite a while ago, before the Second Vatican Council, I had just been ordained a relatively short period of time. I was asked by Father Abbot to give the retreat talks in the retreat house, guesthouse there at Spencer [Abbey]. This is something I always talked about: the Scriptures are a presence of God. We should enthrone the Scriptures in our rooms and go there and find the Lord and listen to the Lord and let the Lord be present to us. So, I shared this with the retreatants. I urged them, "Now when you go home, you enthrone the Bible in your room. Every day come and spend some time and let the Lord speak to you." A priest happened to be on retreat that week. This was back in the pre-Vatican II days. When a priest went to his bishop and told him he was thinking about leaving the priesthood, the first thing the bishop said was, "Now you go on retreat and think that over. You go up to the Trappists for a week." This priest was on retreat supposedly deciding whether he was going to leave the priesthood or not. We had talked a bit during the retreat, so I knew that. I said I would pray for him and I was quite delighted about six months later when he showed up on retreat again, and he was still wearing his Roman collar. I said, "Well, Father, I guess you decided to stay." He said, "Yeah, you know, you hooked me." I said, "*I* hooked you?" He said, "You told me to go home and put the Scriptures in my room and let the

Lord talk to me. When I went home, I got out a little table and put it in the middle of my room, and I put a chalice veil over it, and I put the Bible there. Every time I went into the room, there was the Lord waiting for me. And I started listening to him. I came to know, again, the love I had for him back in the seminary days. Well, I decided to stick it out." He is retired now, but he became a very successful pastor, a much-loved pastor. He is still quite active as the confessor-counselor to a lot of the young priests in the diocese because he was such a wonderful priest.

But he gave God half a chance and the Lord just filled his life with joy and new meaning. That is what Benedict is talking about here. Open the ears, open the eyes. Let the Lord come in through his word. And do it now, *hodie.*[57] *Hodie!* Do not put it off until tomorrow. He says, *Come and listen to me, sons; I will teach you the fear of the* LORD (cf. Ps. 34:12).[58] And the love of the Lord, too. "*Run while you have the* light *of life, that the* darkness *of death may not overtake you*" (cf. Jn. 12:35).[59]

It is interesting how many times in the prologue Benedict uses that word run, *currite,*[60] or "hasten." Or make speed. I wonder how Benedict was. I suspect he was one of those men who hustled around the cloister—really purposeful. He is going to get things done; he does not want to waste time.

In this paragraph [prol. 8–13], Benedict is saying, "Now, you open your eyes and see. You open your ears and listen." But in the next paragraph [prol. 14–21], he turns it around. God is the one. Benedict says:

> Seeking his workman in a multitude of people, the Lord calls out to him and lifts his voice again: *Is there anyone here who yearns for life and desires to see good days?* (Ps. 34:13). If you hear this and your answer is "I do," God then directs these words to you: If you desire true and eternal life, *keep your tongue free from vicious talk and your lips from all deceit; turn away from evil and do good; let peace be your quest and aim* (Ps. 34:14–15).[61]

Now this is God speaking. "My *eyes will be upon you and my ears will listen for your prayers; and even before you ask me, I will say* to you: *Here I am*" (cf. Isa. 58:9).[62] And Benedict comments: "What, dear brothers, is more delightful than this voice of the Lord?"[63] So beautiful!

God is seeking us more than we are seeking him. Benedict makes the primary purpose of the monastic life to truly seek God. He is saying here that God is seeking you and he is calling out to you. Do you want life? Do you want good days?[64] Of course, this is what we all most want from the depths of our being. We want the fullness of life; we want happiness. That is what we are made for.

Benedict is saying, if you say, "Yeah, yeah, I do. I do," then God says, "If you want true and eternal life, *keep your tongue free from vicious talk and your lips from all deceit.*" Reminiscent of Saint James, who says, "The man who controls his tongue is a perfect man" (cf. Jas. 3:2). But more than that. "*Turn away from evil.*"[65] Not only evil of the tongue but all evil. "*And do good.*" Finally, Benedict goes on: "*Let peace be your quest and your aim.*"[66] All of this, of course, is coming from Psalm 34.

Seeking peace is that further step. Not only doing good but seeking that complete tranquility of order. Everything in your life is coming out of trying to live "all things are yours, you are Christ, and Christ is God's" (cf. 1 Cor. 3:22–23). The full order of your life—our whole life—seems to be in complete harmony with the divine will, the divine plan, the divine love.

Seek peace and pursue it. Once you have done this, Benedict says the Lord is going to be right there with you. "Here I am." God is going to be with you: The deep awareness of God's presence, God's love; God is with us. Benedict says, "My *eyes will be upon* you, my *ears will listen* to you, *and even before you ask me, I will say* to you, 'Here I am'" (cf. Isa. 58:9).[67] It is the father of the Prodigal Son. The poor son decides to come back to his father. He has this plan of how he is going to tell his father of how he is sorry, he is going to be his worker and try to merit just some corner. And the father rushes out and embraces him before he can say anything and celebrates him. Just respond the least bit to God's grace, he is more than there. "I am here! I am with you! Here I am!" That experience of the divine presence with us is, indeed, most delightful.

Benedict goes on to say, "See how the Lord in his love shows us the way of life. Clothed then with faith and the performance of good works."[68] This is the basic thing that Benedict is trying to teach. First of all, there has to be the faith. Faith comes through hearing. It is through the Scriptures. Through the enlightenment. The faith that makes us really want God. But then there also has to be the good works. As it says there in Psalm 34, "If you desire to an eternal life, keep your tongue free from evil, your lips from all deceit, turn away from evil, do good. Seek peace and pursue it." There has to be both things. That we really want God, and we do what is necessary for it. The primary thing we need here is to really open ourselves to the experience of the divine love and light. Then our whole heart will be one with God and his will, and we will want to do whatever he wants. Clothed then with faith and the performance of good works, let us set out on this way with the Gospel for our guide, that we may deserve to see him *who has called* us *to his kingdom* (cf. 1 Thess. 2:12).[69] With the Gospel as our guide.

LIVING THE GOSPEL

The plan Benedict sets down in his Rule is only to help us live the Gospel. It is the evangelical life. This is what our [Cistercian] fathers understood so well. I do not know if you have ever read that fascinating letter of Thurstan of York which he wrote to the archbishop of Canterbury talking about the foundation of Fountains Abbey in England.[70] Thurstan quotes Richard of Fountains, the first abbot, the founder. He says, "Most Holy Father, all we want to do is to live the Rule of Benedict, or rather to live the holy Gospels as they are enshrined in the Rule of Benedict." Every time he speaks of it, he speaks in that way. He speaks, "The Rule, or rather the holy Gospels as we are guided in these by our father Benedict."

Thurstan of York says at the end of the letter that what these men are seeking here is exactly what Robert and his men were seeking when they left Molesme and went to start Cîteaux. Richard of Fountain left Saint Mary's of York and went to start Fountains Abbey in much the same way. It was his desire to live the Gospels, to live a life centered on Christ and totally as a disciple of Christ guided by our father Benedict as the sure guide, the wise man, who could guide us in those ways.

What is it all for? Let us set out on this way with the Gospel for our guide that we may deserve to see him *who has called us to his kingdom* (cf. 1 Thess. 2:12).[71] *Ut mereamur erum qui nos vocavit in regnum suum videre.* He has called us. He has called us into his kingdom that we may see him. To see God. That is what the contemplative life is all about. That is what life is all about—to see God. Because when we see him, we shall be like him. We shall be fully and totally deified so that every aspiration that is in our being will be more than fulfilled.

So basically, in this part of the prologue, Benedict is saying, "Wake up! Open your eyes! Open your ears! Let the divine life and light invade you so that your life is filled with aspiration, joy and hope." There is a God who so loves you and wants to give you *everything,* including himself. God wants to bring you into the fullness of divine joy and life. That is what it is all about. When we are in touch with that, there is this deep joy in our being because we have all that we are made for. All that we are called to.

MAY THE DIVINE ASSISTANCE REMAIN WITH US ALWAYS AMEN

VII ❧ SEEKING AND PURSUING PEACE

[14]Seeking his workman in a multitude of people, the Lord calls out to him and lifts his voice again: [15]*Is there anyone here who yearns for life and desires to see good days?*[16] If you hear this and your answer is "I do," God then directs these words to you: [17]If you desire true and eternal life, *keep your tongue free from vicious talk and your lips from all deceit; turn away from evil and do good; let peace be your quest and aim.*

—Prologue
THE RULE OF SAINT BENEDICT

[EDITOR'S NOTE: This talk was given on July 26, the feast of Saints Anne and Joachim, parents of Mary, the mother of Jesus, and grandparents to Jesus. Abbot Basil begins with the story from his life about Saint Anne. Then, he tells about his own grandmothers.]

In my junior year, I was concerned about what I was going to do when I got out of college—kind of searching and wondering if God had anything particular in mind for me.[72] When we finished school that year, I talked three of my classmates, including my twin, to drive up with me and pray at the shrine of Saint Anne. My concern was to ask Saint Anne to help me know what God wanted me to do with my life. Well, she did not waste the opportunity. She made it clear by a number of incidences exactly what God wanted me to do.

A year later, when I graduated from college, she confirmed that it was her doing when, four days after graduating from college, I entered Saint Joseph's Abbey. The practice at that time was a month of postulancy and then you would receive the novice habit the next Sunday. That Sunday for me was the feast of Saint Mary Magdalene, which delighted me. Cistercians have traditionally had a great devotion to Mary Magdalene as one of the great contemplatives. Simple monastic vows were to be made on the Sunday after the completion of your two-year novitiate. It just so worked out that it was the feast of Saint Anne. I guess Saint Anne was claiming her own. So I made my first vows on this feast forty-eight years ago. I have always had a special devotion to Saint Anne in gratitude. I hope that she watches over us all.

SPECIAL GRANDMOTHERS

My grandmothers were special people in my life though they were two diametrically different women. One was extremely strict. On Sunday, we had to spend all day reading the Bible. We could not play; we could not do anything. I remember her at ten o'clock at night, fussing around the kitchen, saying, "There's no rest for the wicked! There's no rest for the wicked!" My other grandmother was an Irish Catholic. She was about much later at night, ironing over the ironing board, saying, "Aye, there's no rest for the weary. There's no rest for the weary." I decided to be weary instead of wicked, so I stayed with the Catholics. Both grandmothers had a great influence on my life.

It was from my Irish grandmother, I think, that I learned contemplative prayer. She took me to Mass when I was little. After Mass she would just sit there. I am sure she was wrapped in contemplation. She would not have even identified with the word, but she would sit quietly for a long time after Mass enjoying the Lord within her. Grandmothers have been a big part of my life, and I am happy about that.

SAINT BENEDICT AND THE PSALMS

We have been looking at the prologue of the Rule. As we come into the second section, we see that Saint Benedict gets down to sort of the brass tacks right from the beginning. He says, What is this all about? He chooses his questions and answers from the inspired word of God. He had a simple faith that this is the *vox divina*, as he calls it, "the divine voice."[73]

First, he chooses from Psalm 34. *Is there anyone here who yearns for life and desires to see good days?*[74] He is touching the basic desire of man. That we want eternal life and are made for eternal life. Death is just an effect of sin. Christ overcame death, and he promises, through the resurrection, eternal life. We want good days. We want life in its fullness.

Benedict also chooses from another psalm. He puts it another way. *Who will dwell in your tent, Lord; or who will find rest upon your holy mountain?* (cf. Ps. 15:1).[75] This is where we will find good days. This is where we will find eternal life. By entering into the kingdom of God. To enter into his tent, to be intimate in his family. To find eternal days.

Benedict has a parallelism here. In each case, he brings forth the answer immediately from the same psalm. So the first time:

> *Is there anyone here who yearns for life and desires to see good days?* If you hear this and your answer is "I do," God then directs these words to you: If you desire true and eternal life, *keep your tongue free from vicious talk and your lips from all deceit; turn away from evil and do good; let peace be your quest and aim* (cf. Ps. 34:13, 14–15).[76]

This is the primary answer that Benedict chooses from the Scriptures to express what the life is all about. It is from Psalm 34. It is something that he heard and prayed again and again. It was a part of his very being as it is ours.

We see here the poetry of the Psalms. God is not just big, God *is*. God is too much to be enclosed in our thoughts and concepts. Therefore, the Scriptures use stories, myths, images, poetry, and metaphors to open into something more. If we are going to understand, open ourselves to the fullness of what the Scriptures are saying to us, then we have to enter into that.

This is why so much emphasis has been placed during the renewal of Scripture studies in the Catholic Church especially, but in all Christian churches, on the literary genre of Scripture. What genre is the Lord using here? You can get ridiculous positions if you take what the Lord is speaking in a myth or story as literal history. It doesn't work. This is what the [current] pope said about [the earlier condemnation of] Galileo: My predecessor was wrong there because he was taking the Scriptures in a literal sense.[77] Therefore, it was thought that everything had to circle the earth. Scripture did not mean to describe how the planetary system works. Rather, it was trying to bring forth this wonderful event of creation in a mythological way. We have to be attuned to genre.

THE POETRY OF THE PSALMS

The Psalms are poetry.[78] Poetry is a way of invoking a response from us to something that is wonderful. It speaks to the deep within us. The Psalms are wonderful poetry. They are able to be transported into different languages because they do not depend on rhyme. Rhyme can be used in poetry, but it can be used tritely. "Now I lay me down to sleep, I pray the Lord my soul to keep, and if I die before I wake, I pray the Lord my soul to take." It has rhythm and rhyme, but is it poetry?

Poetry has a feel, a movement, and it depends on image and metaphor. "The moon was a ghostly galleon tossed upon cloudy seas."[79] Magnificent imagery and rhythm there. You can almost be taken into the experience. You feel yourself in that ghostly galleon, in that whole movement of the clouds and the moon.

The genius of Hebrew poetry is its parallelism. Something is stated and then immediately restated, contrasted, or carried forward in a concrete way. Through awareness of parallelism in poetry, you enter into a deeper, more full experience of the reality.

That is the idea of poetry—to call forth image after image. The example of it is in Psalm 119 in its fullness. You also find it in Psalm 19, which presages what was the delight of the Jewish people—the revelation, the Law and the Prophets. This gift where God has spoken to them and made them his people. The Jewish people love the Torah, the Scriptures, because it is the incarnation of God for them, so they try to express that. In Psalm 119, he has the law. Then he goes on in the next verse, the decrees. Then, the precepts, the commandments, the ordinances, and the word.

If you stop and reflect upon that, you realize in your own spirit: when you hear law, decrees, ordinances, precepts, statutes, the word, you have a different reaction to each. Each word has a nuance. It has an emotional context for you. The idea of the poetry is like circular contemplation—coming at the thing again and again from all different angles until you get a fuller sense of it.

Then in Benedict's descriptions: law is perfect, it is sure, it is right, it is clear, it is pure, it is true, it is desired more than gold, it is sweeter than honey. Each of these images is just filling this out. And as we sing these psalms, it brings us to a fuller appreciation of how precious are the holy Scriptures. It is a place where we encounter God, and God speaks to us, guides us, and guards our life. It is where he shows us the way to the fullness of life.

CONTROL OF SPEECH

Out of all of the possible texts, what is the first one which Benedict chooses as the essence of his Rule? It is the norm, in a sense, for interpreting the Holy Rule. It is very striking. The verse he takes is from Psalm 34. *Keep your*

tongue free from vicious talk and your lips from all deceit.
You have a parallelism there: tongue, lips. Different ways
of expressing the same thing. It is also expressed in Saint
James: A man who controls his own tongue is a perfect
man (cf. Jas. 3:2).

Benedict is conscious of the importance of this in a
community—that we guard our speech well. You have the
two things there—vicious talk and deceit. It is detraction
and calumny. Detraction, or vicious talk, is whenever I
say anything about one of my brothers that in some way
detracts from him. It, in some way, has as its purpose to
cause the other to think less of him, to drag down someone's estimation of him in some way. Calumny, which is
even worse, is when I lie about somebody to bring him
down. This profoundly undermines a community—when
we engage in vicious talk or when we engage in deceit in
regard to one another. That is why it is so important that
we follow the evangelical word of the Lord: if you have
anything against your brother, you first go and speak to
him one-on-one (Mt. 18:15–16). It is a good norm to
keep. You never say anything negative about anyone
unless you have first said it to him face-to-face. You first
go to him. Then the Lord says, if he does not hear you,
bring a couple of brothers.

In the great method of spirituality of our times, the
Alcoholics Anonymous twelve-step program, they call it

intervention. If somebody cannot hear you, you bring a couple others—people he trusts—and together hope that in the testimony of two or three, he will finally hear it. "You've got a drinking problem, brother." Listening to those whom he trusts, he hears the reality of his problem. Only if he does not hear his brothers, then you go to the Church. Then it is time, maybe, for some kind of authoritative action to be taken in order to prevent the man from hurting himself or hurting the community.

Benedict puts this right at the beginning: no vicious talk. Certainly, no calumny. That is the first thing he sees. Then he goes on: turn away from evil and do good.[80] The whole thing of conversion. Not just in turning away from evil of the tongue but all evil, but turning away from evil and doing good. Again, it is a parallelism by contrast— turning from evil, doing good.

The whole of the prologue is summed up in Psalm 1. This whole psalm is engaged in a comparison by contrast. *Happy the man who follows not the counsel of the wicked, nor walks in the way of sinners, not sits in the company of the insolent* (cf. Ps. 1:1).[81] You have a triple parallelism. Each one invites you to a deeper understanding. Do not get involved with evil.

Psalm 1 continues: *but delights in the law of the Lord and meditates on his law day and night* (cf. Ps. 1:2). Another parallelism where it moves into something more concrete. *But delights in the law of the* LORD. How do they express this delight? They meditate on his law day and night. The parallelism of the Hebrew poetry is leading us into a fuller and richer understanding and experience.

He is like a tree planted near running water, that yields its fruit in due season (cf. Ps. 1:3). Again, a parallelism. *Trees planted near running water.* They are fresh. They are vibrant. *That yields fruit in due season.* It goes on to be really fruitful. *Whose leaves never fade. Whatever he does, prospers* (cf. Ps. 1:3). Not only is it always evergreen, but they really prosper in all they do. They are always full of life and leading into fuller life. Then parallelism by contrast: *Not so the wicked, not so; they are like chaff which the wind drives away. Therefore in judgment the wicked shall not stand, nor shall sinners in the assembly of the just* (cf. Ps 1:4–5). Again, a parallelism. They are not standing; they are not involved; they are not a part of the holy community.

Psalm 1 concludes: *For the Lord watches over the way of the just, but the way of the wicked vanishes* (cf. Ps. 1:6). A parallelism by contrast. What he is going to do with the good and what he is going to do with evil. Psalm 1 depicts the whole of the Psalms.

Seeking Peace

Benedict chooses this verse, "They turn from evil and they do good. They seek peace and pursue it" (cf. Ps. 34:15). Again, it is a parallelism. Seeking peace. How do they seek peace? They *pursue* it. There is an energy, there is a wholeness of a being put into it. This is the way Benedict summarizes our whole monastic life: to keep your tongue free from vicious talk and your lips from all deceit; turn from evil and do good; seek peace and pursue it.[82]

Traditionally, over the centuries, the model of Benedict and his Rule has been *pax*. You find *pax* or *pax intrantibus* over our gate, and you find these over the gates of many monasteries. "Peace." "Peace to those who enter here." Peace. Aquinas speaks of it as the tranquility of order. Everything is in a serenity, in a movement, in a rhythm, in a harmony—being a complete *yes* to God. *Blessed are the peacemakers because they shall be called sons of God* (cf. Mt. 5:9). *Called* as in the Scripture sense—it is a *calling* which actually brings into being. We are *called* into being. By being men of peace, we truly become the sons of God, become one with Christ in God. That is why Benedict could sum up the whole of the life. First of all, getting away from any kind of talk that could eviscerate the community. Then, seeking peace and pursuing it. Seeking to be in complete and total harmony with each other and, above all, with God.

Benedict sums up by first taking from Psalm 34 and then from Psalm 14. They complement each other. He has been so formed by Scripture, as all our own Cistercian fathers and mothers. They are filled with Scripture and reflect Scripture in the way they think. Although Benedict makes many practical, concrete decisions in the Rule—he speaks about discretion of the abbot, discretion in practicing the Rule, the freedom of the abbot to adapt the Rule to the community—the basic guide for interpreting the Rule is to be this primary thrust which Benedict draws from the word of God and sets forth in the prologue. It is important to reflect deeply (enter into) and receive the fullness of what God is saying in his word: keep your lips from any kind of vicious talk and any kind of deceit, turn from evil and do good, seek peace and pursue it.

MAY THE DIVINE ASSISTANCE AMEN
REMAIN WITH US ALWAYS

VIII ❧ PARALLELISM IN THE RULE

¹⁴Seeking his workman in a multitude of people, the Lord calls out to him and lifts his voice again: ¹⁵*Is there anyone here who yearns for life and desires to see good days?* ¹⁶If you hear this and your answer is "I do," God then directs these words to you: ¹⁷If you desire true and eternal life, *keep your tongue free from vicious talk and your lips from all deceit; turn away from evil and do good; let peace be your quest and aim.*

²²If we wish to dwell in the tent of this kingdom, we will never arrive unless we run there by doing good deeds. ²³But let us ask the Lord with the Prophet: *Who will dwell in your tent, LORD; who will find rest upon your holy mountain?* ²⁴After this question, brothers, let us listen well to what the Lord says in reply, for he shows us the way to his tent. ²⁵*One who walks without blemish,* he says, *and is just in all his dealings;* ²⁶*who speaks the truth from his heart and has not practiced deceit with his tongue;* ²⁷*who has not wronged a fellowman in any way, nor listened to slanders against his neighbor* (Ps. 15:1, 2–3).

—Prologue, THE RULE OF SAINT BENEDICT

Let us get back to the prologue of the Holy Rule. Last time, we got into parallelism in the psalms. Parallelism is the very essence of Hebrew poetry. We talked about how one verse is followed by another verse which in some way seeks to bring us to a fuller experience of it—to emphasize it, repeat it in another way, call forth other images, show the contrast, and show the concrete possibilities. And so Benedict, like all of our fathers—Cistercian fathers and all of the Church fathers—was profoundly formed by Scripture. When he comes to writing his prologue, Benedict enters into the nature of parallelism. He writes with parallelisms and chooses psalms that have parallelisms.

After reminding us that prayer is fundamental to the beginning of every good work,[83] Benedict goes on to say what life is about. He asks the same question in two different ways, using different psalms. First he goes to Psalm 34: *Is there anyone here who yearns for life and desires to see good days?* In the next paragraph, he goes to Psalm 15: *Who will dwell in your tent, LORD; who will find rest upon your holy mountain?* Here the question is given more concretely using the image of the Lord's tent. If you want the fullness of life and to see good days, where is this to be found? Of course, in the tent of the Lord and the house of God.

In response to the first question [yearning for life and good days], Benedict answers with a psalm and parallelism.

Keep your tongue free from vicious talk and your lips from all deceit; turn away from evil and do good; seek peace and pursue it (cf. Ps. 34:14–15). Each one moves in a progression.

In the next paragraph, he uses Psalm 15 to answer the second question, *Who will dwell in your tent,* LORD*; who will find rest upon your holy mountain?* The answer: *One who walks without blemish and is just in all his dealings; who speaks the truth from his heart and has not practiced deceit with his tongue; who has not wronged a fellowman in any way, nor listened to slanders against his neighbor.* There are three parallels in that psalm.

One who walks without blemish. Now immediately, what parallel Scripture comes to mind for us? The Lamb without blemish, right? (1 Pet. 1:19).[84] The sacrificed Lamb. The Lamb of God, Jesus. What Benedict invokes for the Christian is the one who walks in Christ's way.

Is just in all his dealings. This brings out more concretely what must be done to dwell in the Lord's tent. *Just* in Hebrew is *sedek*, which means more than what we would usually mean by "just" or "justice." It means "the whole rightness of the order." "Righteousness" is the word we used in the past, but it is now archaic and has tones we do not like so much. This is the way our Lord expressed it: "I seek always to do the things that please the father" (cf. Jn. 8:29). It means to be in complete harmony with the divine will. There is a christological meaning here that Benedict would have been aware of in calling us to fullness of life.

Who speaks the truth from his heart and has not practiced deceit with his tongue. Benedict comes back to speech—the idea of the lips and the heart in harmony. Our words are not just on our lips but in our hearts. When one speaks the truth, there is no deceit. We are whole; there is integrity there. Benedict later applies this to prayer, but here he speaks of the psalmody in particular. In chapter nineteen ("The Discipline of the Psalmody") of the Rule, what is the phrase Benedict ends with? In Latin style, it is that last word—that last phrase—that underlies the whole. What is the one he has there? *Mens concordet voci.*[85] That the inner spirit is completely in harmony with the voice when we pray the Psalms. It applies to every aspect of the life. There is both this truth within us and the truth that comes forth.

Who has not wronged a fellowman in any way, nor listened to slanders against his neighbor. This is a parallelism with Psalm 34, *keeps his tongue free from vicious talk and lips from all deceit.* Here Benedict brings it a step further. He doesn't even listen to the stuff. Actually, the Latin word is *accepit,* meaning he does not accept. He does not go along with this stuff at all. *Neighbor* is a word with strong connotations for the

Christian. It is the story of the good Samaritan (Lk. 10:30–37). Who is your neighbor?

ZEAL TO AVOID SLANDER

Slander in the Rule is the translation of the Latin *opprobrium*. In Scripture, *approbrium* occurs from time to time and it is usually translated as slander.

Benedict uses *opprobria* in chapter fifty-eight when he is talking about the qualities you are looking for in the man in coming to the life.[86] Does he have zeal for the work of God, zeal for obedience, and zeal for this *opprobria* [translated as "trials"]? Translators and commentators have struggled with this. What is Benedict really talking about? Many appeal to a place in the Rule of Saint Basil where he puts together the three: the work of God, obedience, and a humble way of life.[87] This interpretation is probably the most common understanding of what Benedict is saying. It corresponds to the path of holiness that Benedict traces out in the steps of humility.[88] The first two steps are about the *Opus Dei*, the praise of God, and the next three steps are about obedience, followed by four steps about humility.

I wonder, though, if it could be a legitimate interpretation here that Benedict is saying: zeal for the work of God—really be zealous about praising God and entering into the prayer; zeal for obedience—completely like

Christ, "I do always the things that please the Father." And when he speaks about zeal for *opprobria*, he means zeal to avoid this vice of *opprobrium*—slander, calumny, and detraction.

If Benedict makes avoiding slander so capital at the very beginning of his Rule, it would not be surprising that this would be one of the things he would look for in the person who comes to the monastery. It is the person who does not speak evil of others—does not detract or talk calumniously about others—but has zeal to stay away from all of that.

GUARDING THE TONGUE IS WISDOM

In the prologue, Benedict is laying out the principles for his Rule. The first thing he says is pray. We expect that. It might seem strange, however, to see what comes next. He shows his primary concern about slander, detraction, and calumny. We would maybe choose some beautiful text from Scripture about charity and love. But when Benedict was writing this, he was an old man with a lot of experience. He was writing out of that experience. He is saying that this is the thing where monks can most easily destroy and undermine the bond of charity, the communion of love in the community: by slander, detraction, and calumny. This is what you have to watch out for, first of all. Then you can go on to seek peace and pursue it. Then you can go on to be like the unblemished Lamb, a sacrifice who does always the things that please the Father, who is truly the just man. It is something worth pondering.

Benedict is setting the principles for hearing and interpreting the provisions of the Holy Rule. It is important that we understand this wisdom of Benedict. What are the principles, insights, and wisdom of Benedict? A lot of the details of the Rule we cannot follow today. For a number of the details, Benedict says, let the abbot decide that, or, the abbot can change if he sees well.[89] When we commit ourselves to live according to the Rule of Saint Benedict, it is not to live according to all of the details but to live according to the divine wisdom that is found in this Rule that expresses the Gospels in a powerful and effective way. It is a Rule that has guided millions through centuries.

What are the Scripture texts he is drawing upon to give the first impetus, the first look, at his Rule? He says, first of all, watch out for this stuff—detraction, calumny, and slander—saying anything evil about anyone. Then go deeper into your heart and allow none of it in your heart. Clean this all up, and *then* you are ready to seek peace. In fact, this is the way you come to "seek peace and pursue it."[90] Then you are ready to walk with the unblemished Lamb and to come to true justice.

It is very powerful when you reflect on what Benedict writes at the beginning of the Rule to set the tone. From all the Scriptures, he has specifically chosen these two passages from the Psalms. Ponder and try to understand more fully the spirit he is trying to give here when he says, "Do not speak anything evil. Turn from evil and do good. And then go on to seek peace and pursue it." Peace is the fullness. Who seeks life? Who wants the fullness of day? Seek peace and pursue it. Who wants to live in his tent? It is to walk with the unblemished Lamb and to come into all justice, all righteousness, and to be in complete harmony with the divine will. A beginning place is the cleaning up. This goes back to Saint James: The man who guards his own tongue and keeps it from evil is a precious man (cf. Jas. 3:2).

It is the real challenge that our love and care for each other leads us to purify our hearts, minds, and lips. That we speak only well of each other, support each other, encourage each other, and do everything we can to help each other to live in the fullness of this. Like Jesus, we seek always to do the things which please the Father. Let us seek peace and pursue it, together as a community and then each as an individual. And it all comes together in Christ.

MAY THE DIVINE ASSISTANCE AMEN
REMAIN WITH US ALWAYS

IX ONE WITH CHRIST

⁴¹What is not possible to us by nature, let us ask the Lord to supply by the help of his grace. ⁴²If we wish to reach eternal life, even as we avoid the torments of hell, ⁴³then—while there is still time, while we are in this body and have time to accomplish all these things by the light of life— ⁴⁴we must run and do now what will profit us forever. ⁴⁵Therefore we intend to establish a school for the Lord's service. ⁴⁶In drawing up its regulations, we hope to set down nothing harsh, nothing burdensome. ⁴⁷The good of all concerned, however, may prompt us to a little strictness in order to amend faults and to safeguard love. ⁴⁸Do not be daunted immediately by fear and run away from the road that leads to salvation. It is bound to be narrow at the outset. ⁴⁹But as we progress in this way of life and in faith, we shall run on the path of God's commandments, our hearts overflowing with the inexpressible delight of love. ⁵⁰Never swerving from his instructions, then, but faithfully observing his teaching in the monastery until death, we shall through patience

*share in the sufferings of Christ that we may deserve
also to share in his kingdom. Amen.*

—Prologue

THE RULE OF SAINT BENEDICT

In the beginning of the prologue Benedict speaks of us as sons, which is our most formal title, the greatest thing about us. We *are* sons of God, baptized into Christ, made the very sons of God. But as he continues in his teaching, Benedict speaks of us as *carissami fratres,* "my most dear brothers, my dearest brothers."[91] He is with us on the journey. We are all sons together—sons of God.

INTIMACY WITH GOD

Benedict speaks from the depths of his own experience. He said, "Who wants life?"[92] Well, we all want life. "Who wants to see good days?" We all want happiness. That's what we are made for. He says, "Who wants to dwell in the tent of God?"[93] That is where eternal life is. That is where eternal joy is.

Benedict uses, again and again, that word *tent* rather than temple or house. He uses those at times, but *tent* speaks of a certain intimacy—to share somebody's tent. He was profoundly influenced by the Scriptures, and the Scriptures are formed of that Middle Eastern ethos—the hospitality of the tent. You welcome somebody into your tent. You dwell in intimacy with God. "Who wants this?" asks Benedict, and then he gives us the simple, straightforward answer of the Scriptures. Guard your mouth and then guard your heart; turn from evil, turn to good; seek peace and pursue it.[94] Seek the fullness and completeness of being in harmony with God and with everyone else and everything else.

Having been given that word of life—that instruction to us—Benedict talks about the fruit of it, the results of it. The first thing he brings out is: Now when you do this, God is going to listen to you.[95] This is going to be a two-way street. There is going be this intimacy—this friendship—and God is going to listen to you. "Once you have done this, *my eyes will be upon* you *and* my ears *will listen* for your *prayers; and even before you ask me I will say* to you: *Here I am* (Isa. 58:9)."[96] God is going to be so much with us. If we seek him—*seek and you shall find* (cf. Mt. 7:7–8)—we will find him and there will be this intimate living together in his tent. He will hear us; he will be with us; he will share life fully with us.

Benedict goes on to say: "What, dear brothers, is more delightful than this voice of the Lord calling to us?"[97] Have you ever had the experience of really wanting something or wanting to do something, yet you cannot figure out how to do it? You cannot find a way to do it. Then someone comes along and says, "Oh, this is the way to do it," and they show you the way. There is real joy. Now I can get it! Now I can do it! That is what Benedict is talking about. Do you really want life eternal? Do you want full happiness? Do you want eternal joy? Here is the way. You say, "Now I can do it. I can have it. I can attain it." That is why he has found immense joy because he really experienced this. He had the way to eternal life. For Benedict, so fundamental to all of this is the way of humility.

DEFEATING THE DEVIL

Benedict has a bit of irony also found in Scriptures. He takes the delight, too, that they are foiling the devil. You fooled the devil. He thought he was going to get you. He is not going to get you now because you have the way. To be able to do this, know this, and experience this is God's gift.

These people *fear the Lord*, and do not become elated over their good deeds, they judge it is the Lord's power, not their own, that brings about the good in them. *They praise* the Lord working in them, and say with the Prophet: *Not to us, Lord, not to us give the glory, but to your name alone* (cf. Ps. 115:1). In just this way Paul the Apostle refused to take credit for the power of his preaching. He declared: *By God's grace I am what I am* (cf. 1 Cor. 15:10). And again he said: *He who boasts should make his boast to the Lord* (cf. 2 Cor. 10:17).[98]

CHRIST THE ROCK

Benedict will develop this in the Rule: to be very conscious that if we can do any of this, if we can hear any of this, if we can learn any of this, if we can understand any of this, it is by God's grace, his gift. It is completely God's gift.

Benedict shows that, even though he has used many texts from the Hebrew Bible, he is completely centered in Christ. "That is what the Lord says in the Gospel: *Whoever hears these words of mine and does them is like the wise man who built his house upon rock* (cf. Mt. 7:24)."[99] The rock is Christ. It is by hearing Christ's words and living them that we build ourselves solidly on Christ. That is the stability that he speaks of in the Rule. It is founded on Christ, on the Rock. Benedict is centered in Christ here and throughout the Rule. He is constantly bringing it back to Christ.

TO BE AN EXAMPLE FOR OTHERS

Now that he has given this basic insight, Benedict brings it to a certain conclusion. "With this conclusion, the Lord waits for us daily to translate into action, as we should, his holy teachings."[100] Benedict shows that this is his own lived experience. He speaks about life being lengthened. Here is an old man who has been on the journey a long time. Why the longevity of life? he asks.

In the Buddhist tradition is the idea that once a man arrives at a certain enlightenment, he does not always immediately pass into nirvana.[101] Sometimes he is left here in a state of what they speak of as bodhisattva—left here to be an example, to be an encouragement, to be a teacher for others. Benedict is bringing out a part of that here. Why is this life prolonged? So that we can live life more fully and be an example, a witness, a teacher, a source of strength to those coming after.

This is something all of us older monks need to be aware of. The Lord sends us many fine young men, and we want to hand on to them the rich heritage that is ours in this beautiful abbey and this wonderful life. But the only way to hand it on is by really living it and welcoming them into the lived experience of it. You do not learn the monastic life by words or teaching and hearing about it. The way you enter monastic life is by living the life.

You hear the stories among the fathers of the desert that a young man will come to a father and say, "Father, how can I be a monk?" The abba will say to him, "Just watch me and do what I do. Get up when I get up. Work when I work. Sleep when I sleep. Pray when I pray. Eat when I eat." Just by doing that, the young monk is brought into purification of the heart, inner peace, deep prayer, and the experience of God.

We come into this monastic life and we live it. The older ones live it and create the matrix which the younger ones can enter and come to know by *experience* what it is to be a true monk, a true Cistercian, a true follower of Saint Benedict. This life is prolonged not just for our own sake. It is also prolonged so that we can be a source of life for others and pass on the wonderful gift that we have received.

Benedict comes back to what he said in the first part. "We must, then, prepare our hearts and bodies for the battle of holy obedience to his instructions. What is not possible to us by nature, let us ask the Lord to supply by the help of his grace."[102] The obedience, the prayer—the things he spoke of at the beginning.

Having brought this together, the basic thrust of it, then Benedict says: "Therefore we intend to establish a school for the Lord's service."[103] For those who really want full-ness of life, want good days, want to come to dwell in the tent of God, we are going to set up a school, a place where we can learn how to live into this.

Benedict speaks about the school: "In drawing up its regulations, we hope to set down nothing harsh, nothing burdensome."[104] He may be thinking of the *Rule of the Master*, which he was probably brought up under, or some of the other early rules which were harsh and cer-tainly burdensome.[105] Benedict did not want any of that, but he says that nonetheless, it is going to be tough at the beginning. It is going to be tough because it involves conversion. It involves leaving things behind, disciplining oneself: getting up early, spending time in prayer and work in service to the community—trying to discipline one's mind and one's heart.

"The good of all concerned, however, may prompt us to a little strictness in order to amend faults and to safeguard love."[106] It is to amend our faults, but also to safeguard love. Benedict speaks a great deal there, drawing from Scriptures, about the dangers of calumny, detraction, and slander. So he will establish certain norms for silence to safeguard love. That is his concern. He says, "Do not give up. Do not run away. Do not be daunted. It is bound to be narrow at the outset."

"But as we progress in this way of life and in faith, we shall run on the path of God's commandments, our hearts overflowing with inexpressible delight of love."[107] This is a teaching found in all monastic traditions: be faithful to your practice. Illumined by faith, you enter into and follow the practice. That is the great dimension here. All traditions have different expressions for faith. By living the practice in faith and trust, what will happen in living the practice? You will come to the sweetness of an unutterable love. What happens in the monastic life is that through *lectio*, through the *Opus Dei*, through the sharing among the brethren, we come to know God, to really love God.

And when you really love someone, you find delight—a real joy—in making them happy and being with them. I am sure most of you have had the experience sometime in your life, when you are in love with someone, what a joy it is to find ways to please them. You try to find out what is their favorite food, their favorite thing they like to do. You find joy in bringing surprises and pleasure into their life. So it is as we grow in this life. We find joy because we are more with God in love. Like Jesus, we only want to do the things that please the Father (Jn. 8:29). We find a real joy in that. There is a deep joy in knowing that I am pleasing God, and I am walking with God. I am doing the things that delight him. That comes about when one grows in this life. This growth in love comes day by day as we are faithful in the way. So Benedict says our hearts are overflowing with the inexpressible delight of love.

Share in the Sufferings of Christ

"Never swerving from his instructions, then, but faithfully observing his teaching in the monastery until death, we shall through patience share in the sufferings of Christ."[108] Again, you hear an old man, here: "through patience." Not just old men, but everyone is to be patient

91

with God's slow progress. It is God's work. He is going to bring it out, but he does it at his pace.

Patience with ourselves. Again and again, we fail. We do not quite do it and we don't act the way we want to act. We don't think the way we want to think. We just struggle along. Then, patience with our brothers. These guys whom we love, we see goofing up, too, by doing things or not seeing things.

Patience with God. We know that God could do it all like that, but he wants us to have the glory of walking, working, and struggling with him. So, Benedict says that it is through patience that we share in the passion of Christ.

As Jesus walked toward Jerusalem he prayed, *My soul is troubled now, yet what should I say—Father, save me from this hour? But it was for this that I came to this hour. Father, glorify your name!* (cf. Jn. 12:27–28). He knew what lay ahead and he wanted to get over with it, but he had to take it step by step. He had to go through the whole thing. As Jesus hung on the cross for three hours—some say less, others say it was five hours—it must have seemed like an eternity. In all the agony, waiting for it to be over, so he could say, "It is finished," and give up his spirit (Jn. 19:30). Benedict invites us to enter the patience of Christ in his passion.

Why did Christ endure the passion and completely follow the Father's plan in it even though parts of him begged to be let off? *If it be possible, Father, let this chalice pass me, but not my will, but your will be done* (cf. Mt. 26:39; Lk. 22:42). Why did he do all of this? For love of you and for love of me. For love of each one of us. We, too, through patience, share in the passion of Christ for the redemption of this world. In our love for Christ, we want to be with him in his sufferings, in his ministry, and in his mission of saving the world. Through patience we share in the passion of Christ. We must be willing to go on and on, one day at a time.

Finally Benedict finishes: *ut et regno eius mereamur esse consortes*. "That we may deserve to share his kingdom."[109] We will share his patience, his passion, and his kingdom. In classical Latin, as I have mentioned before, the most important word is always placed last. Everything leads up to it. And the last word that Benedict wrote in his prologue is *consortes*. *Consortes Christi*. "Heirs with Christ." In English, we have the word *consort*. What is a consort? It is the woman chosen by the king. Whether she be a poor commoner or a princess, he has chosen her to share all of his royal dignity and power—even his royal body. She is the one he has chosen to enter most fully into all that he has and is as king, ruler, master, emperor.

By baptism, we have already been brought into a oneness with Christ. To share totally Christ's being, his life, his goodness, his joy. *Consortes. Sortes* is the lot. *Con*, share.

Share the lot. The whole of this—the whole of the Rule, the whole of the plan, the whole way of life—is for this: that we may most fully enter into our call to be the consorts of Christ. Even that word is not strong enough as it is in the reality, in the case of Christ, to be absolutely one with Christ.

Jesus prayed at the Last Supper, *so that they may be one just as we are* (Jn. 17:11). We know that the Father and the Son are absolutely one even though they remain distinct persons. We, too, are called to an absolute oneness with Christ even though we remain distinct persons. This means to be called fully into the inner life of the Trinity. The divine love poured by the Father upon the Son is poured out upon us. The Holy Spirit as the love of God becomes our spirit, and one with Christ, we cry out, "*Abba*, Father!" (Rom. 8:15).

This is what we do in contemplation. We just sit there and let the divine love—this total torrent of divine love—completely pour upon us. We receive it and have the capacity to receive it because we have been Christ-ed. With that love, we are a perfect response to God, the Father.

This is what Benedict sees: to come to the freedom and the realization to know who we are, be who we are, and be that in the fullness. That is what the life is about for Benedict. That is where we run with hearts expanded with the sweetness of a divine love. Benedict knew this life in his own experience and wanted it to be an experience for all of his disciples—a life that was filled with *intense* joy, *intense* happiness. It was already experienced by Benedict, and it was constantly moving him into a fuller experience of the divine union—being one with Christ, to the Father and the Holy Spirit.

I have spent days with that one word, *consortes*. Called to be the consort. The English word isn't enough. We are to be one with Christ, to have Christ bring us into the fullness of who he is, into the fullness of his divine delight, in the transforming union in the Trinity. As Benedict brought out, it is only by God's grace that we come into this light, this understanding, and this living. So we humbly and earnestly pray, "Lord, open my mind. Open my heart. Open my being. Pour in your light, your grace, that I may know who I am and be who I am and live in the fullness of who I am." As a *consortes Christi*. As one who is totally with Christ in all that he is in God.

MAY THE DIVINE ASSISTANCE AMEN
REMAIN WITH US ALWAYS

X ❦ THE KINDS OF MONKS

¹*There are clearly four kinds of monks.* ²*First, there are the cenobites, that is to say, those who belong to a monastery, where they serve under a rule and an abbot.* ³*Second, there are the anchorites or hermits, who have come through the test of living in a monastery for a long time, and have passed beyond the first fervor of monastic life.* ⁴*Thanks to the help and guidance of many, they are now trained to fight against the devil. . . .* ⁶*Third, there are the sarabaites, the most detestable kind of monks, who with no experience to guide them, no rule to try them as gold is tried in a furnace (Prov. 27:21), have a character as soft as lead. . . .* ¹⁰*Fourth and finally, there are the monks called gyrovagues, who spend their entire lives drifting from region to region, staying as guests for three or four days in different monasteries. . . .* ¹³*Let us pass them by, then, and with the help of the Lord, proceed to draw up a plan for the strong kind, the cenobites.*

—Chapter 1
THE RULE OF SAINT BENEDICT

I received in the mail a manuscript from Liturgical Press in Collegeville, Minnesota, titled *The Manhattan Psalter*.[110] You might recall, about a year and a half ago, we received the death notice of Sister Juanita [Colón], a sister of Wrentham [Mount Saint Mary's Abbey in Massachusetts]. Sister Juanita was a fairly young nun, full of life, very vivacious. When she was diagnosed with cancer, it hit her very hard. She was told that she would die in a relatively short time. When Mother Agnes asked if there was anything special that she would like at her funeral, Sister Juanita said, "I want a pair of green dancing shoes, so when I get to heaven, I can dance." So Sister Juanita was buried in green dancing shoes. Probably the first Trappistine that ever was.

As Sister Juanita faced this ordeal of death, she turned, in a very traditional Cistercian way, to the Psalms. She spent hours with the Psalms. She began to rewrite the Psalms in her native Manhattan lingo. The Psalms may have lost some of their poetry, but they certainly got to be much more down-to-earth and earthy. She went through the whole psalter three times and was going through it the fourth time when she died.

At her wake, we prayed the psalms using her Manhattan version. Many people were struck by them, and so the Benedictines of Liturgical Press asked if they

97

could publish them. They sent a manuscript to me asking for a recommendation or a blurb, as they call it.

We were looking at the prologue. Remember that Saint Benedict, seeking to present the essence of the monastic life, himself turns to the Psalms. Following the spirit of the Psalms in Hebrew poetry, he uses parallelism, so he takes first some verses from Psalm 34 and then Psalm 14. First from Psalm 34:

Is there anyone here who yearns for life and desires to see good days? If you hear this and your answer is "I do," God then directs these words to you: If you desire true and eternal life, *keep your tongue free from vicious talk and your lips from all deceit; turn away from evil and do good; seek peace and pursue it.*[111]

Benedict takes the fundamental question from Psalm 34 and then gives a program for monastic life. Well, this is the way that Sister Juanita expresses this:

Is it a long life you want? Security?

Imagine what a poignant question that was for a young woman who is facing death.

LISTEN WITH YOUR HEART

Then watch your tongue! Let every word you say be true. Every action open and above board. Avoid bad company. Always try to do the right thing. Be peaceable, always trying to find peaceful solutions to the problems of life.

It is down-to-earth. It was certainly what she was struggling with, trying to find a peaceful solution to undoubtedly the biggest problem of her life: facing a very painful death from cancer as a young woman.

Benedict then goes on to Psalm 15.

O Lord, who shall sojourn in your tent? Who shall dwell on your holy mountain? He who walks blamelessly and does justice; who thinks the truth in his heart and slanders not with his tongue; who harms not his fellow man, nor takes up a reproach against his neighbor (vv. 1–3).[112]

The way Sister Juanita expresses that was:

Lord, please tell me. What must one do to earn admission into your inner circle? My real friends are right living, obedient, and sincere, says the Lord. They do not gossip with others or about others, recklessly destroying good names and reputations. They are loyal and do not hold grudges, but willingly and generously forgive wrongs. They do not consort with scoffers but are always first to show respect for a man of God.

It is refreshing and invigorating to hear the Psalms set forth in a New York way. They should make good *lectio,* especially when you listen to them in the context of this young woman who was seeking to draw out of the Psalms the strength, consolation, light, and courage to walk peacefully to death. A painful death at a young age.

In the prologue, Benedict puts forth the essence of monastic life—to seek peace and pursue it;[113] to dwell intimately with God in his house.[114] The text here is interesting. There are various manuscript versions of the Rule, but at the end of the prologue, most have the words, "Here begins the text of the Rule." The RB 1980 has an interesting parenthesis which is not found in other versions. "It is called a rule because it regulates the lives of those who obey it."

The word *rule* was just coming into its own. There were actually many rules. The early ones were in Greek, followed by as many as eighty in Latin.[115] They were usually just documents, testaments, question-and-answer things like Saint Basil's, which the head of the monastery, or the head of the monastic group, wrote to guide monks and pass on wisdom. The Master [who wrote the *Rule of the Master*], who was just before Benedict, wrote a long and, in many ways, a harsh rule.[116] The Master used this word *rule* to describe the guidelines he established for bringing order out of the chaos often created when monks lived together in the common life.

Benedict follows the *Rule of the Master* but says in the prologue that he does not want to keep the harshness that is there.[117] Rather, he wants to bring a way that leads to the excitement and joy which comes from the experience of divine love. That, of course, is what our Cistercian fathers were looking to in wanting to live this Rule to the full.[118] A monastic rule regulates the life of monks. *Regulate* comes from the same word as *rule*.

Benedict's first chapter is about the kinds of monks. He begins with a bold and direct statement. "There are clearly four kinds of monks." Your first reaction is, "Now wait a second. I know a lot more than four kinds of monks. There are all kinds of monks." And you could start naming them off. But it is obvious that Saint Benedict is using this in the teaching moment.

Benedict establishes, as he says at the end of the chapter, that the way of monastic life which he is legislating for—the cenobitic life—is the *fortissimum*, "the strongest."[119] It is the way of monastic life most able to strengthen us and help us grow in living out the fullness of monastic ideals. Benedict does not spend much time on the cenobitic life in this chapter since his whole Rule is about it. He is, however, warning us about three of the most common movements, or devious ways, that draw us away from living the monastic ideal to the full. He draws a concrete picture of them.

In presenting the kinds of monks, Benedict indicates why he chose the three particular vows given in chapter fifty-eight of the Rule: stability, fidelity to monastic life, and obedience.[120] He calls upon the man who really wants to enter into the life to make these three promises, or vows.

First, There Are the Cenobites

Benedict says, "First, there are the cenobites."[121] A cenobite is a transliteration of a Greek word, *koinos bios*—the common life. The essence of cenobitic life is that we live a common life, walking together. We are strengthening each other; we are supported by each other. Together we learn the way of truth and humility.

In chapter seven of his Rule, Saint Benedict has the living of the common life as the eighth rung in the ladder of humility. "The eighth step of humility is that a monk does only what is endorsed by the common rule of the monastery and the example set by his superiors."[122] We do nothing but what the Rule and the example of the seniors call us to.

So the first kind of monks are the cenobites. "That is to say, those who belong to a monastery."[123] They belong to a community. *Belong* is not the correct translation of the Latin. They are "monastery men" is the way it says it in the Latin.

Militans sub regula vel abbate. "Fighting under the rule and the abbot." The quip on this is, "Yeah, the monks are always fighting." Again, Benedict is back to his military terminology—carrying on the campaign; going forward. *Sub regula vel abbate* in the earlier Latin was understood as a rule *or* an abbot, but in the later Latin it came to mean the rule *and* the abbot. Benedict obviously means *and*, since he insists on both the rule and the abbot throughout his teaching.

Those Who Live Apart

Benedict comes to the second kind of monk. "Second, there are the anchorites."[124] It is a Greek word meaning "for those who live apart," or "hermits." *Eremo*, those who live in the desert.

"Who have come through the test of living in a monastery for a long time, and have passed beyond the first fervor of the monastic life." In Latin, it means rather the novitiate fervor, the fervor of the novice in the life.

Thanks to the help and guidance of many, they are now trained to fight against the devil. They have built up their strength and from the battle line in the ranks of their brothers to the single combat of the desert. Self-reliant now, without the support of another, they are ready with God's help to grapple single-handed with the vices of body and mind.[125]

As Benedict writes this, I think he has a bit of tongue-in-cheek. This is where he parted from Cassian.[126] He looks to Cassian very much for spiritual teaching, and he urged that each evening the community gather before compline and read or listen to some of Cassian.[127] In chapter seventy-three, Benedict points to Cassian as one whom we should go to for the richer and deeper teaching. Cassian idolized the hermits in the desert, but for Benedict the cenobitic way was more fruitful.

I think, too, that Benedict is poking a little fun at himself. Remember how Benedict started out. When he had his conversion he did go off by himself, and he got into that cave. He lived apart all by himself, even to the extent that he did not even know when was the feast of Easter.[128] He had so separated himself from the Church and, in a sense, from Christ. This made him "prefer absolutely nothing to the love of Christ."[129]

As we know from Saint Gregory, Benedict had a hard time in that cave with the flesh. He ended up having to roll himself in thorn bushes.[130] He had a hard time with his thoughts and the thoughts provoked by the way people acted around him. That eventually is what drove him from the cave and made him seek a cenobitic community.

So, in a way, I think that Benedict is poking fun at the eremitic life. He emphasizes the vices of singularity and self-reliance in what he describes as single-handed combat. The monk is standing out there on his own rather than entering into communal life.

THE MOST DETESTABLE KIND OF MONKS

Benedict speaks of the third type of monk, the sarabaites.

> Third, there are the sarabaites, the most detestable kind of monks, who with no experience to guide them, no rule to try them *as gold is tried in the furnace* (Prov. 27:21), have a character as soft as lead. Still loyal to the world by their actions, they clearly lie to God by their tonsure. Two or three together, or even alone, without a shepherd, they pen themselves up in their own sheepfolds, not the Lord's. Their law is what they like to do, whatever strikes their fancy. Anything they believe in and choose, they call holy; anything they dislike, they consider forbidden.[131]

This is the way of self-will. Benedict, in one of the instruments of good works in chapter four, says we are to make ourselves strangers to the ways of the world.[132] Here, Benedict is saying that sarabaites are still loyal to the world in the way they act and live. Benedict is rather moderate in his descriptions of the types of monks. He just has two or three sentences. Actually, the *Rule of the Master* had over sixty sentences in describing sarabaites.

We all are in danger of becoming, in some way, sarabitic. We choose our own ways and decide what is good and bad according to our likes and dislikes. In a large cenobitic community, the abbot is shepherding in a general way. He tries to inspire, call forth, and lead the community the best he can, but he cannot have that kind of intimate touch with everybody in the community. Some will come to him and he will keep close to them. But there is a great danger when one begins to be more and more on one's own. In the novitiate, the novice works closely with the novice master. As a junior, the monk works with the junior master. It is very important to have someone always in our lives as a spiritual guide—a spiritual friend—who knows us intimately. Someone with whom we are completely open and who advises, encourages, challenges, questions, and warns us. Otherwise, we are in great danger of becoming our own guides.

WALKING WITH ANOTHER

No longer having a shepherd, penned up in our own little pen, living the way we are comfortable with, and making our own judgments can lead to a pious life in the cloister, but not to living the way of the Rule to the full so we come to experience that unutterable sweetness of the way of divine love. I do not think anybody could hope to do that unless he has somebody with whom he is walking closely on the journey. It is extremely important that each of us finds someone in the community as a spiritual friend, spiritual companion, spiritual brother, spiritual father—I do not care what you call them—but somebody who we are really open with and will allow to challenge us so that we do not come into this sarabitic way of thinking.

"Anything they believe in and choose, they call holy; anything they dislike, they consider forbidden." That's what I like, that is good. Instead of this, we are here to follow the Good Shepherd, to be in his flock. We need to hear his voice and we need to hear it clearly. And we need help to hear it. That is what makes the cenobitic life the *fortissimum genus*, the kind that most strengthens us. It gives us brothers to walk with on the way. It gives us spiritual fathers. It gives us an abba. I think it is why Benedict puts it right there, to warn us that there is always this danger of going off on our own.

I worked with thirty-six experimental foundations in the late 1960s and the early 1970s. These are people who have gone off in twos and threes and singularly to start their own monastery and lead their own community in their own way. I would dare to say that almost all of them are sarabitic. You judge a tree by its fruit. I would not go as far as Saint Benedict in calling these experimental groups as the "most detestable kind of monks," but I do think, at least, it is one of the unfruitful ways of monasticism.

Most of us will have no temptation to go off and start our monastery, either alone or in a group of two or three, but we have to constantly watch ourselves *within* the community. Are we constantly seeking to be led by the Good Shepherd, Christ the Lord, rather than being led by our own likes and dislikes? From my years of experience, the only way is to allow someone in on it. You are in danger if you are doing anything that you do not want to share with anybody. You do not want to let your spiritual father know about it. You don't want to "expose it to the light" and talk about it. That is a warning. What is going on here?

Openness with the spiritual father is the greatest assurance that we will be encouraged and strengthened to follow the Good Shepherd. We will be challenged and kept safe from doing anything that would not be strengthening and helping us to live to the full what we want to do as men who truly seek God and want to run in the way that leads to the divine sweetness.

MAY THE DIVINE ASSISTANCE REMAIN WITH US ALWAYS AMEN

XI ❧ LOVERS OF BRETHREN AND PLACE

¹There are clearly four kinds of monks.
—Chapter 1
THE RULE OF SAINT BENEDICT

We were looking at the first chapter of the Holy Rule where Benedict tells us there are four kinds of monks. It is a structure he uses as a teaching method to show how the cenobite is the strongest kind of monk—strongest in the sense that the cenobitic life strengthens us to live to the full what we want to live as monks. Benedict then looks at the other kinds of monks and shows how they fail in that. The anchorite, or hermit, does not have the strength of the brethren. He has to stand, so to speak, on his own two feet. That certainly demands a lot more of a person and makes it difficult for prayer. When one is supported by the brethren he has a much better chance of being faithful to his ideals and not deceiving himself. And then a second group, the sarabaites, are monks who have the *propriis voluntatibus* or "self-will." They do their own sweet will instead of the common will—the will we share with Christ and God. They have their own ideas.

Whatever they think is good is good, and whatever they think is not good is not good. They have self-will.

Benedict then goes on to the fourth group of monks; he calls these gyrovagues. It is made up of a Greek word and a Latin word. *Gyro* is the Greek word meaning round and round, as in a gyroscope. *Vagues* is somebody who has no rooted place. He has no home. He is just a vagrant. Gyrovagues are people who do not root anywhere. They are just going here and there. As Benedict says: "They spend their entire lives drifting from region to region, staying as guests for three or four days in different monasteries. Always on the move, they never settle down, and are slaves to their own wills and gross appetites. In every way they are worse than sarabaites."[133] They are at the bottom of the ladder.

In the literal sense, there are not many gyrovagues in our time. I know a couple of them. One was wandering through monasteries in Africa after he wandered through all of the monasteries in the United States and the Caribbean.

Through these types of monks, Benedict is pointing out the tendencies in all of us. We have to be watchful of them. One of these tendencies is instability, not so much in body but in mind. Rather than coming to dwell within the monastery, we are unsettled. It is the kind of person who is looking for every reason to go out—shopping, visiting, taking care of this, that, and the other thing. They are always wanting new scenery and to see new things.

In the Cistercian tradition especially, but in other monastic traditions as well, the monastery is supposed to be a beautiful place—beautifully located with beautiful buildings. It is to be a sacrament of the divine beauty. But it is a beauty that does not distract but draws us more and more deeply into itself, year by year. We come to settle deeply in the divine presence—the divine beauty—rather than being constantly distracted by new sights, new images, and things to see and experience. This is what the gyrovague is looking for. We can be gyrovagues without leaving the monastery by wanting to hear the latest news, spending time with newspapers, magazines, novels, travel books, and video cassettes. We are traveling within the monastery itself rather than allowing ourselves to settle in the quietness, peace, and the beauty of it—a place where our mind and heart can find true rest in the divine.

PATIENCE TO BECOME SETTLED

This takes time. We have all grown up in a world that is immensely rich in all sorts of things. I remember one day, years ago, I was at my nephew's house. They had just been blessed with another little boy who was about two months old at the time. The mother had to go shopping and asked, "Would you watch him?" I said, "What do I do?" She said, "Oh, you don't have to do anything. Just watch him." She sat him in front of the television and turned on the television. Two months old and he is sitting there for a couple of hours just watching the television. She said the doctor said that is good. It stimulates the growth of his eyes and mind. I am thinking, from the time you are two months old you are watching television for hours. What a collection of stuff you have in there! Even if you enter the monastery at twenty years old or twenty-five, or if you have been out in the world for thirty, forty, or fifty years, it takes a long time for things to settle. It is like a pond after a tornado or a typhoon. We had typhoons at Lantao in Hong Kong where everything would be washed up on shore and the sea would be a murky mess for days. Only gradually did it settle again and become clear and placid. So it takes time to settle in a monastery and allow the beauty and serenity to gradually draw us in. As we let go of some of this stuff, we become more settled.

Benedict has then described these four kinds of monks: cenobite, anchorite or hermit, sarabite, and the gyrovague. He uses the kinds of monks to teach us awareness of these tendencies in us: singularity, self-will, and instability. Singularity is in Benedict's eighth step of humility.[134] It is the monk who wants to stand out.

This is deep in us, too. In our society, we are impelled into developing this false self which is made up of what I do, what I have, and what other people think of me. We want to do things and have things so that we stand out. We see all sorts of outlandish things—red, spiked hair, earrings, and nose rings. People, in a superficial way, are trying to stand out. Others, in a deeper way, try to stand out through their work, for example. The monk in the common life seeks to settle down and blend with the others.

THE EXAMPLE OF THOMAS MERTON

When Merton was at Columbia University, he was the bright young man on campus. The yearbook was filled with pictures of Merton. He happened to be the editor of it, but he was always doing things to stand out on campus. So when he entered the monastery, he was going to be *the* monk. Saint Bernard, in his commentary on the steps of humility, describes this kind of monk. Merton felt it fitted him in some ways.

Until maybe thirty or forty years ago, the monks had no access to mirrors whatsoever. There were no mirrors in the monastery. The brothers wore beards, but the fathers were shaved by somebody else.[135] Traditionally, they were shaved seven times a year. It became more frequent until finally the priests were allowed to shave themselves. I remember Merton writing about the day he was presented with a shave brush, creme, razor, and a little mirror. He looked at his face for the first time in years and was shocked.

Saint Bernard is writing this in the context of somebody who does not have a mirror.

When a man has been bragging that he is better than others he would feel ashamed of himself if he did not live up to his boast and show how much better than others he is. The common rule of the monastery and the example of the seniors are no longer enough for him. He does not so much want to be better as to be seen to be better. He is not so much concerned about leading a better life as appearing to others to do so. He can then say "I am not like the rest of men." He is more complacent about fasting for one day when the others are feasting than about fasting seven days with all the rest. He prefers some petty private devotion to the whole night office of psalms. While he is at his meals he casts his eyes around the tables and if he sees anyone eating less than himself he is mortified at being outdone and promptly and cruelly deprives himself of even necessary food. He would rather starve his body than his pride. If he sees anyone more thin, anyone more pallid, he despises himself. He is never at rest. He wonders what others think about the appearance of his face and as he cannot see it he must only guess whether it is rosy or wan by looking at his hands and arms, poking at his ribs, and feeling his shoulders and loins to see how skinny or fleshy they are. He is very exact about his own particular doings and slack about the common exercises. He will stay awake in bed and sleep in choir. After sleeping through the night office while the others were singing psalms, he stays to pray alone in the oratory while they are resting in the cloister. He makes sure that those sitting outside know he is there modestly hidden in his corner, clearing his throat and coughing and groaning and sighing.[136]

If you have ever seen a picture of Merton around 1949 or 1950, he looks like somebody out of a concentration camp. He so starved himself that he ruined his digestive system, ended up in the hospital, and spent the rest of his life on a special diet. It is the sort of thing that sarabaites do—special things to stand out. Benedict is warning against this "standing out" in different ways, including virtuous acts. Sarabaites are trying to stand out and be their own self rather than enter into, as Bernard speaks there, the common way lived by the community. It is the instability of always looking to do different things.

THE MONASTIC VOWS

Benedict's description of the types of monks helps explain why he chose the vows for the monks.[137] The vow of obedience is against the sarabitic way of one choosing his own will. The vow of stability is against the instability of the gyrovague who is always moving around looking for new and different things. Then, the vow of *conversatio morum*, "a continual transformation of the mind and heart according to God's plan for us."[138] This vow of the common, cenobitic way of life is contrary to the singularity of the eremitic or anchorite life.

Benedict is setting the tone for the kind of monastic life that he believes is the strongest. It is the type of life which will most strongly support us in moving ahead to live the fullness of monasticism which he describes in the prologue. It is the way which leads one to just run, as he says, in the way of the delights of the divine love.[139] Having traced that out—the cenobitic life—Benedict looks at the abbot and community.

It is a challenge for all of us to constantly watch ourselves for tendencies to singularity, self-will, and instability. Meditating on the types of monks in the first chapter helps us understand the meaning and significance of the vows we are called to—their value and their power in our lives. These vows help us to live what we really want to live in truly seeking God and finding that complete freedom of the sons of God—to be in the divine and not to be pulled about by these basic, vicious tendencies within us.

LOVERS OF BRETHREN AND PLACE

The earliest Cistercians described monks as lovers of the brethren and the place.[140] This sums up the cenobitic life. Lovers of the brethren means knowing these brothers that the Lord has given us. We have this great support to live to the full what we want to live in a world today where so many people are without support. Even very wealthy people find themselves alone in the end, but we are surrounded by a loving community that is going to support us all of the way. They will always be with us on the journey. What a tremendously precious thing is this cenobitic life. To be lovers of the place is the awareness of the beauty of what is set up to support us in living what we want to live. Everything about it is there to take care of us and enable us to fully enter into contemplating God. The Cistercians expressed the cenobitic life in this positive way—to be lovers of the brethren and the place.

MAY THE DIVINE ASSISTANCE REMAIN WITH US ALWAYS AMEN

XII ❧ JESUS CHRIST IN THE ABBOT AND COMMUNITY 🜍

> [1]To be worthy of the task of governing a monastery, the abbot must always remember what his title signifies and act as a superior should. [2]He is believed to hold the place of Christ in the monastery, since he is addressed by a title of Christ, [3]as the Apostle indicates: You have received the spirit of adoption of sons by which we exclaim, abba, father (Rom. 8:15).
>
> —Chapter 2
> THE RULE OF SAINT BENEDICT

In the beginning of the second chapter of the Rule, Saint Benedict says the abbot is believed to hold the place of Christ in the community.[141] *Is believed.* I do not know whether it is harder for the abbot or the brethren to believe that!

The point of it is: we are all Christ. We have all been baptized into Christ. *It is now no longer I that live, but Christ lives in me* (cf. Gal. 2:20). We are all called to be Christ. When you stop to reflect on that, it is kind of a scary thing, a humbling thing. I am supposed to be

Christ? This poor, weak, stupid sinner who falls and fails in so many ways? Yet, this is the way Christ has chosen to be in the world today.

Benedict speaks of the abbot as the *maioris*—the "superior"—one who kind of stands out in the community in both position and quality of life.[142] That is what I think he is saying. We are all to be Christ, but this one in particular because we have chosen him to be the leader of the community. The abbot has to, in some way, be an image of Christ—to be clearly Christ in the community.

JESUS CHRIST IN OUR MIDST

A story comes from Poland about a monastery that was dying. There were just four monks left, but they were good monks—very observant, trying to keep choir going. They had a little hermitage on the property, and one day the local rabbi, an elderly and holy man, came to the monastery and asked if he could use their hermitage for his retreat days. The monks said, "Yes, you are most welcome. We don't use it that much." So, the old rabbi went out to the hermitage.

One day the four monks were discerning what God wanted of them—where they were going to go, what the future was for this monastery. They came up with the idea, "Why don't one of us go out and ask the rabbi?" One of the monks went to the hermitage and asked the rabbi. The rabbi said, "I really don't know what you should do, but I can tell you this much. The Messiah is in your midst." The monk went rushing back.

"Do you know what he said? He said the Messiah is in our midst!"

The four of them looked at each other and looked at themselves. They said, "Who is he talking about? The prior? The porter? Guestmaster? The cook? Which one?" It changed their whole way of interacting as each thought of the other; he might be the Messiah. There was a new reverence, appreciation, and openness for each other. Soon the guests who came to the monastery saw that and they told others about it. More and more people starting coming. Then young men started applying. And the community grew and flourished again.

Christ is in our midst. If each one of us first looked at himself and said, I am Christ in the midst. It is my responsibility to bring Christ's presence into this community. To bring Christ's love to each one of these men. To be an experience of Christ for them and begin living out of that.

Each one here is Christ. The Lord makes that so clear in the Scriptures. *Amen I say to you, as long as you did it for one of these, the least of my brethren, you did it for me* (cf. Mt. 25:40). If I really worked at that consciousness: this is Christ who is next to me in choir. This is Christ who I work with. This is Christ who I serve. This is Christ whom I speak with. Yes, the abbot holds the place of Christ, but Christ is in all of us.

I think it would make quite a difference if all of us consciously worked at that—trying to be truly present to ourselves as a Christ-person and then constantly reminded ourselves, each one is Christ.

RESPONSIBLE, ONE FOR ANOTHER

On my retreat days, I often take out a community list. I go down the list and ask myself, How is each one doing? Today, I could ask the question, How have I experienced Christ in each one? How have I been Christ to each one?

When we join the community, we take on a great responsibility. When a man gets married, he takes on the responsibility of a wife. Then they may have children for which they are responsible. But when we join the community, we take on the responsibility for every single member of the community. Saint Benedict is very strong in regards to the abbot. He is going to have to answer for the obedience of every member of the community.[143] But it is not just the abbot. When we become a part of this cell in the body of Christ, we take on a real responsibility for each and every member of this body. Each one takes responsibility for the others. The enormous blessing and grace of cenobitic community life is that I have all of these brothers who have a loving concern about my well-being, my growth into Christ, and about my being all that God wants me to be.

Benedict says that absolutely nothing be preferred to the love of Christ.[144] That's the bottom line. The reason we care for Christ in ourselves and in each other is because we care for Christ. And if we do not care for Christ in ourselves and in each other, how can we say that we really care for Christ?

FILLED WITH JOY

What joy we can have! I really love Christ, and when you love somebody, you want to do something for them. In the community you have all of these opportunities to do something for Christ because anything you do for any of your brothers, or anyone, it is for Christ. *Whatever you did for one of these, the least of my brethren, you did it for me* (cf. Mt. 25:40). We can have the joy of a fulfilled love in caring for each other, bringing joy to each other, supporting each other, and affirming each other.

Christ is the heart-center of our community and of our lives. We live because of Christ Jesus. He is the source of our lives. He is the way, the truth, and the life (Jn. 14:6). He is the word from whom all things were made (Jn. 1:1–3). Everything comes from him, and everything goes back to him. The more we are living in the fullness of that, and the consciousness of that, the more wonderful our life is. The more it is filled with joy. The fruits of the Spirit—charity, joy, peace, patience, kindness, goodness, generosity, gentleness, faithfulness, modesty, self-control, chastity—are all there (Gal. 5:22–23).

The abbot is believed to hold the place of Christ in the community, but so is everyone else. It is the faith we try to build up each day in our *lectio,* prayer, reflections, and *meditatio.*[145] Through faith we rise to that higher level of consciousness—Christ consciousness. Then will our life be filled with joy. The story about the little Polish monastery has a lot of truth in it. When people see the radiant life, love, care, and joy that is here, then we can be sure that this monastery will be what we want it to be—a powerful center of spiritual life and witness of the awareness of Jesus Christ.

MAY THE DIVINE ASSISTANCE AMEN
REMAIN WITH US ALWAYS

XIII ✦ THE RESPONSIBILITIES OF THE ABBOT

¹To be worthy of the task of governing a monastery, the abbot must always remember what his title signifies and act as a superior should. ²He is believed to hold the place of Christ in the monastery, since he is addressed by a title of Christ, ³as the Apostle indicates: *You have received the spirit of adoption of sons by which we exclaim, abba, father (Rom. 8:15).* ⁴Therefore, the abbot must never teach or decree or command anything that would deviate from the Lord's instructions. ⁵On the contrary, everything he teaches and commands should, like the leaven of divine justice, permeate the minds of his disciples.

³⁰The abbot must always remember what he is and remember what he is called, aware that more will be expected of a man to whom more has been entrusted. ³¹He must know what a difficult and demanding burden he has undertaken: directing souls and serving a variety of temperaments, coaxing, reproving and encouraging them as appropriate. ³²He must so accommodate and adapt himself to each one's character and intelligence that he will not only

keep the flock entrusted to his care from dwindling, but will rejoice in the increase of a good flock. [33]Above all, he must not show too great concern for the fleeting and temporal things of this world, neglecting or treating lightly the welfare of those entrusted to him.

—Chapter 2
THE RULE OF SAINT BENEDICT

I think abbots go back frequently to chapters two ("Qualities of the Abbot") and sixty-four ("The Election of an Abbot") of the Holy Rule. I have been spending some time with them—praying and pondering. With the novices this morning, we were looking at a letter written by our [Cistercian] father Saint Stephen at the presentation of the first Cistercian hymnal.[146] They used the hymnal of the monks of Molesme at first, but in their desire to really live the Holy Rule, they sought to have a hymnal more in accord with the directives of the Rule. This short letter gives insight into how much Saint Stephen and the other founders looked to Saint Benedict and the Rule for their guidance.

Saint Stephen loved the liturgy, and he was concerned that the liturgy be authentic and in line with the Rule. He studied Hebrew to make sure the biblical text—the psalms—were accurate. He sent monks to Metz because they supposedly had the best chants for Mass. Then he sent monks down to Molesme to get the hymnal of Saint Ambrose. Of course, Benedict spoke of the Ambrosianum.[147] When Stephen had put this hymnal together, he promulgated it, saying:

> Brother Stephen, the second superior of the New Monastery, sends greetings to his successors. We command the sons of Holy Church that these hymns, which it is certain that the Blessed Archbishop Ambrose composed, and which were brought to this place, namely, the New Monastery, from the Church of Milan, where they are sung, *these alone and no others,* henceforth must be sung by us and by all our posterity; and indeed, our Blessed Father and Master Benedict, in his Rule, which we have decreed must be observed in this place with great care, prescribes that these same hymns be sung by us. Wherefore, by the authority of God and our own authority, we enjoin upon you that you never presume through levity to change or detract from the integrity of the Holy Rule, which you know has been worked out and established by us in this place with no little labor, but rather, living as lovers, imitators, and defenders of our holy Father, *you hold* to these hymns inviolably.[148]

"Living as lovers, imitators, and defenders of our Holy Father." You see the great concern to draw from the Rule the wisdom to live by. Our Cistercian founders had a great love for this great, wise man, Benedict. So we turn to Benedict, again and again, for the guidance we need. The monks saw the Rule as their way to live the Gospels, to follow Christ.

When Benedict speaks about the abbot, this is the first point he makes:

> To be worthy of the task of governing a monastery, the abbot must always remember what his title signifies and act as a superior should. He is believed to hold the place of Christ in the monastery, since he is addressed by a title of Christ, as the Apostle indicates: *You have received the spirit of adoption of sons by which we exclaim, abba, father* (Rom. 8:15).[149]

We are here because somehow, some way, at some point, we came to realize who we are—men who are baptized into Christ, who are Christ-persons. The real meaning and the fulfillment of our lives is precisely in being who we are. For some of us, it may have been a moment of great enlightenment. For others, it may have been something gradually seeped into our consciousness. It is not in amassing great wealth, having beautiful homes, having people think well of us—for they will die as quickly as we do—and accomplishing things. Essentially it is in being Christ today in the world. Living the Christ-life to the full. Living to the fullness of who we are as men baptized into Christ. That is the meaning of our lives.

Somehow or other, we wanted a place where we would have maximum freedom to do that, and the greatest possible support to do that. Somehow we came to know that is what you can find in a Cistercian monastery. Here, the life is totally structured to give us the greatest possible freedom to live the Christ-life. We have a community of like-minded men who are seeking the same thing and want to support us to live it to the full.

THE ABBOT AS CHRIST'S PRESENCE

So we come to this community to live the fullness of our Christ-person. Therefore, the head of this community has to be Christ. Nothing else would make any sense but that Christ be the head of our community, the guide. We are incarnate, so in some way Christ is incarnate in our midst. That is what Benedict is saying about the abbot: he is the one who holds Christ's place in the midst. He is to be the Christ, leading and guiding the community. The abbot should be conscious of this being what he is called to be.

He is believed to hold the place of Christ in the monastery, since he is addressed by a title of Christ, as the Apostle indicates: *You have received the spirit of adoption of sons by which we exclaim, abba, father* (Rom. 8:15).

In the context of Saint Paul's letter to the Christians in Rome, the text is referring to God the Father, with Christ saying, "*Abba*, Father." But Benedict is applying it here to Christ as our abba, as our father. Benedict does that deliberately. A true father has, you might say, a double role. He is the one who generates, brings into being, but he is also the one who educates. He brings the one he has brought into being into the fullness of his manhood, the realization of who he is. Until fairly recent times, people did not go to schools. It was the father and the home and the family who educated the sons. He showed his trades to his sons. He helped them learn how to be men, fathers, and husbands—to raise a family. So abba meant not just the generative but also the educative function.

The Abbot as a Spiritual Father

From the beginning of Christianity, we find spiritual fathers. These were men who were not generative of the physical life but of the spiritual life. They were the abbas

130

of the desert. This is the point Benedict is making here in referring abba to Christ rather than to God the Father. We look to Christ as our teacher, our master, the abba who generates us by his teaching, by giving us the fullness of his own life. This is done not by generating life as God the Father, but by his teaching, wisdom, and by the word. The seeds that he sows come through his words.

The abbot is abba in that sense. He is there to be the spiritual father. He generates life in the community and each member of the community by bringing them the word of life—the seeds given by Christ in his teaching and revelation.

Benedict goes on to say, "Therefore, the abbot must never teach or decree or command anything that would deviate from the Lord's instructions."[150] The Latin is *extra praeceptum Domini*, "outside of the teaching of the Lord." Everything the abbot is doing is to be within the context of Christ. It is to be Christ within Christ's way of leading, guiding, and instructing. Christ is the one, and the abbot is simply a sacrament of Christ who brings Christ's word—Christ's generative word—to life in us.

CHRIST'S WORDS AS A LEAVEN

Benedict says, "On the contrary, everything he teaches and commands should, like the leaven of divine justice, permeate the minds of his disciples."[151] Justice there does not mean law and order. Justice here is in the sense of the fullness of righteousness, proper ordering. The divine justice is the way in which God orders the creation.

Leaven is used in making bread. A little bit of leaven in the flour and water permeates the whole and lifts it up. It makes the dough lively. You beat it down, and it will come back up. It is only when you bake it that you finally kill the leaven. In the pioneer days, the pioneers would take a handful of sourdough and mix it with water and flour to make bread. Then they would take just one handful and put it away for the next day. They would carry it across the country. Each day this bit of leaven would be used to make sourdough bread.

Benedict is saying that the abbot's teaching is just a tiny element of the monastic life. The whole life is forming us: the liturgy, our fraternal communion, our work, the beautiful monastery, the creation around, our *lectio*, our communion with Christ, the Office. All of these form us, but in their midst is to be this leaven which is Christ's teaching sown by the abbot.

Now, *mentibus* here is not just the intellect as we think of mind, but it is the whole spiritual dimension—the mind and the heart. The abbot is to sow this word which will be a leaven of divine justice and righteousness. It is to be in the mind and the heart of each of the disciples to lift him and cause him to expand with the divine energy, the divine joy, and the divine life. Even when he gets beaten down, it is going to be there to lift him up again. So it is constantly there. This is the first responsibility that Benedict sees of the abbot: to be sure that the living word of Christ, which is the seed of the divine life, is sown into the minds and hearts of the monks, the disciples of Christ.

Benedict says the abbot has to do this as much by example as by word.[152] That is the enormous challenge for the abbot. He is to be Christ in word and in deed.

THE GOSPEL AND THE RULE

I was sharing with the novices a letter written by Archbishop Thurstan of York. He was writing an account of the founding of Fountains Abbey.

> We ought to recall what happened in the affair of the Molesme monks, which is quite similar. The Cistercians went forth to establish and found a most perfect way of life. . . . They faithfully undertook a renewal of the Holy Rule and a total living of it. . . . Indeed, it is clearer than light that in their wonderful way of life the truth of the whole Gospel shines forth.[153]

> We think of the monks of Savigny and Clairvaux who recently came to us. The Gospel so clearly shone

out in them that it must be said it would be more useful to imitate them than to recite it. When, indeed,
their holy life is seen, it is as if the Gospel were being
relived in them. . . . Happy, indeed, are men such as
these whose clothing, food, and whole way of life
savor the Gospel.[154]

They identified living the Rule of Saint Benedict with
living the Gospel. The situation at Saint Mary's of York
was similar with Molesme. At Molesme, when Robert,
Alberic, and Stephen and their followers were planning to
live the Rule more completely, they got into trouble with
the brethren. The same happened at Saint Mary's of York.
It was a Benedictine abbey, so the abbot was kind of out
of it. He lived in a palace and did the social affairs. The
prior, Prior Richard, was the one who ran the community.
He was also the one who was leading the reform.
Thurstan expresses these reform ideas:

They were men who were determined to correct
their way of life according to the Rule of Saint
Benedict, or rather, according to the truth of the
Gospel.[155]

All of them are seeking full observance of the Rule
and of their profession and likewise of the Gospel.[156]

[T]hese men who wish truly to obey the Gospel of Christ and the Rule of Saint Benedict.[157]

Thurstan quotes Richard speaking to the abbot:

We must undertake with all our strength to observe by God's grace the true and age-old service of our blessed Father Benedict, or rather the more ancient Gospel of Christ which precedes all vows and rules.[158]

Saint Benedict acknowledges as his own only those who live in a monastery under a rule and an abbot, so, venerable Father, if you will allow, we will hasten back to the purity of the Gospels, to evangelical perfection and peace.[159]

He is saying that the Rule and the Gospels are the things of life.

When Richard and his confreres tried to bring about this renewal at Saint Mary's, they ran into trouble. Thurstan of York tried to mediate in the chapter, but the brethren rose up in arms. Thurstan and the monks had to flee down the cloister, into the church, barricade the door, and escape out the back door. Thurstan took them home to his palace and eventually they went and founded Fountains Abbey.

We come to live the Rule of Saint Benedict as a way of living the Gospels. Therefore, our whole life is centered on Christ. The abbot is to see the community as led by Christ and centered on Christ. This is the leaven which animates him and gives vitality to the whole of our life.

ACCOUNTABILITY

During the first couple of months as your abbot, I tried to listen to the members of the community to get a sense of what we wanted, needed, and what the Lord was calling us to. Then we made this long list, and I asked the community to prioritize it. The highest priority chosen was that of accountability. As I read this chapter of the Rule on the abbot, I thought of how Benedict constantly comes back to accountability. Immediately, he tells the abbot, you are fully accountable to the Lord.[160] This is his lot, not your lot. You are shepherd and you are accountable to the Lord for everything that goes on here.

It struck me, as I was looking at this chapter, how much the idea of accountability is written into the Rule of Saint Benedict. As Benedict comes towards the end of his chapter—and he has so many things to say there about the relationship of the abbot and the community— he gives a summary.

The abbot must always remember what he is and remember what he is called, aware that more will be expected of a man to whom more has been entrusted. He must know what a difficult and demanding burden he has undertaken: directing souls and serving a variety of temperaments, coaxing, reproving and encouraging them as appropriate. He must so accommodate and adapt himself to each one's character and intelligence that he will not only keep the flock entrusted to his care from dwindling, but will rejoice in the increase of a good flock. Above all, he must not show too great concern for the fleeting and temporal things of this world, neglecting or treating lightly the welfare of those entrusted to him.[161]

One in Christ

Being abbot is quite a task. I depend very much on the prayers, the love, and the support of each one of you to carry that out. I will try to be there for each one of you in the best way I can. We are a very rich community—a wonderful richness of persons and personalities. There are a real variety of temperaments, too. So we can come to a powerful mix—a powerful presence—by being a community alive in love, care, and compassion. I delight in that. I really want to serve you in every way I can and as Christlike as I can, but I really depend very much on you.

Yesterday, I was with a group of men who are here on a vocation discernment. I shared with them and invited questions. One of the young men asked, "If monks don't do so much talking to each other and have all of these times of silence, how do you come to be so united in love?" It was a perceptive question. We communicate on different levels. What we communicate and what we express in an extraordinary, powerful way in our solemn vows is our commitment to each other in Christ. We are committed to be together in the Divine Office, in silent prayer and meditation, and at the celebration of the Eucharist. We realize more and more profoundly, even though we may not too readily articulate it, that we are one in Christ. We all have been baptized into Christ. We are seeking to live to the full as men who have been Christ-ed. Therefore, we are men who are truly one. We live in the reality and experience of it. It is a source of something very deep and real within as individuals and as community. It is this that I want to see, more than anything else, grow and be a deep and profound joy to us all.

Let us center completely on Christ, put our trust in him, and ask him to take care of us in all our needs at this time.

MAY THE DIVINE ASSISTANCE REMAIN WITH US ALWAYS AMEN

XIV ❦ THE GLORY OF WORK

¹Idleness is the enemy of the soul. Therefore, the brothers should have specified periods for manual labor as well as for prayerful reading.

⁸When they live by the labor of their hands, as our fathers and the apostles did, then they are really monks.

—Chapter 48
THE RULE OF SAINT BENEDICT

Chapter forty-eight of the Rule is on daily manual labor. Benedict begins it by saying, "Idleness is the enemy of the soul."[162] So we do not have to struggle, we should keep busy. Benedict therefore plans the day to be filled with *lectio* [spiritual reading] and labor. He has already spoken about the Divine Office and the meals—the times we gather as a community. But how do we use the time that is not taken up in communal prayer and being together in chapter and the refectory? He says we should fill it with *lectio* and labor. Very few of us would be capable of spending the whole time in *lectio*—really seeking God in the Word and reading—so Benedict sees labor as one way of keeping idleness away. Labor, however, means so much more than that.

LABOR IN MONASTICISM

Benedict says later in the chapter, "Then they are truly monks when they live by the labor of their own hands as our fathers and the apostles."[163] Saint Paul boasted about earning his living making tents; he was never living off other people (Acts 18:3).[164] The Desert Fathers in Egypt even weaved baskets for work. When there was a famine in Alexandria, the fathers of the desert sent food that they had raised to the city.

We have a Cistercian hermit in the mountains of Norway. He makes his living by weaving baskets out of the roots of birch trees. I said to him, "How, way up in the mountains, do you market this?" He said, "When I have a half a dozen or so baskets, I leave them down by the side of road with a note saying, 'Please deliver this to this shop in Oslo.' They always get there. The woman in the shop in Oslo deposits the money in my account at the general store, and I can get my supplies when I need them." I was amazed.

The wonder of our life in community is a certain co-dependence. I use co-dependence not in the modern psychological sense of the term—an unhealthy co-dependence. Rather, it is a healthy co-dependence where we depend on one another. Father John may not be baking fruitcakes at the bakery or turning out stained glass, but if he was not getting the food and cooking the meals, none of us would be doing it either. We depend on each other. Brother Gabriel gets our clothes done; Brother Alan keeps the place heated on these cold days; and Brother Alphonse sees that we have water to drink. We all work together. Together we have this dependence on each other. It is wonderful.

There is another dimension to work that our faith brings in. Sometimes it sounds like piety. People say, "If only I could have just been at the workshop at Nazareth and help Jesus. Help him carry the beams. Help him do his carpentry work." But the fact is that we all have the opportunity to help Christ. Jesus said, *As long as you did it for one of these, the least of my brethren, you did it for me* (cf. Mt. 25:40). Everything we do for each other, whether it is cleaning the house, cooking the meals, taking care of the sick, making the fruitcake, or doing the laundry—whatever it is—we are having this joy. If we really love Christ—and we do—we find a great joy in our work. Whatever the work, there is a joy there because we are able to do this for Christ, with Christ, and be Christ doing it for the others. There is a wonderful reality there.

BEING CO-CREATORS

Another dimension of the work, which means a lot to me, is that God has entrusted us to be co-creators with him. We are called upon with him to bring this creation to its completion and fullness. Everything we do, creative and constructive, is part of bringing creation to its fullness. It is obvious to some, like the brothers building this magnificent church. I just had supper with one of the guests [in the retreat house] who, although he had been here before, said, "That church! This morning the light coming through the windows at Lauds and Mass. . . ." He was speechless. It is a magnificent church, and when you build a church like that, you can be aware of co-creating with God.[165]

We are doing something wonderful in this creation. In any work we are doing, and in every work we are doing, even if it is washing the toilets or raking leaves, we are working on what is the most important: bringing to its fullness and beauty the most important thing, namely, ourselves—you and me. We are the greatest thing in creation. We are the very image of God. In God's plan, we were made in the image and likeness of God. We show forth the tremendous beauty of God, but that likeness was lost by sin, and we went into the region of unlikeness. We are coming back into true likeness, a union and communion with God.

One of the great blessings and wonders of obedience is to know that I am doing what God wants me to do. When I am doing something in obedience, I know this is where God wants me to be working with him right now in bringing this creation to its fullness. The inner dispositions are extremely important. That is where I have to work at it—of being wholeheartedly there with Christ doing this work and celebrating it. Work has a wonderful way of bringing us to the reality.

FACING OUR LIMITATIONS IN WORK

I can remember in my early days as a monk at Spencer [Abbey], when I worked in the vegetable garden. In those days, we tried to raise all of our own food. You would go to the garden and begin work, but after going along about ten feet you would then suddenly hit a stone. You'd say to yourself, "Well, I have to get that stone out." So you start digging. But after a while, you'd begin to think you have found the top of Mount Everest! You'd spend the whole afternoon digging, and still not get that blessed stone, which is a boulder, out of the earth. The work just brings you to your limitations.

Nowadays it happens on a computer. You are typing your way and suddenly something goes wrong and you lose a whole week's work. You cannot get the blessed thing to work the way it should. This is what happens in work again and again. We suddenly get confronted with our terrible limitations. We are brought to our complete dependency on God.

As Benedict says, Whatever you do, begin with most fervent prayer.[166] Half the time, we forget that, and we charge right into our work. But before the work is over, we are praying, Lord help me! It is a real dependence on the Lord because of our limitations.

Work is really a wonderful thing. We can become co-creators with God and co-redeemers with Christ. This is the primal penance that God gave man when man fell. God said, *In the sweat of your brow you shall eat bread* (cf. Gen. 3:19). That penance is united with Christ's passion, death, and resurrection as a redemptive force for the whole world. Even when the work is tough, it is still wonderful because here we are with Christ saving this world.

THE GIFT OF WORK

Work is where we can serve each other—really be there for each other. And allowing others to serve us is a wonderful aspect of this oneness. It brings us to the fact that we are one. We depend on each other; we are in this together.

We spend a fourth of our waking hours in work, and many others a good bit more. Work is an important element of our life, so it is good for us to reflect on its full meaning and significance. It is not just a job to get done.

It is wonderful that we have the gift of work, but we are only going to have it so long. We have to face the fact of diminishments. Of course, our dear Father Lawrence is proof to the opposite.[167] He is still working at ninety-four, going strong down at [preparing the] bonsai [trees], doing the dishes after our meals, and cutting the cherries for the fruitcake at the bakery. Father Charles is at the welcome center giving people joy and a "good ear" of listening. Father Luke has us all in good clothes. I just gave him another job. So it is wonderful that we are able to keep going.

I was in the infirmary talking with Abbot Gus today. He cannot do manual work anymore, but he still contributes to the community. You go into his room, and he just radiates with that smile. He lifts up your spirit. It is wonderful to be able to be and work with God. That is what Gus is doing. He is still working with God and creating a beautiful Gus and a lot of other beautiful people, too. Through work we have the opportunity to be with God in the creating and the re-creating, saving the world, and serving each other.

Yes, work is our primal penance. During these days of Lent, it is good to think about that aspect of work. But we are uniting with Christ in saving the world. There is so much to rejoice about in our work—the joy and the privilege of it. While we enjoy our *lectio,* we can also enjoy our work. Even if it is cleaning your room. Several of the seniors have said, "Every day I work on cleaning my room." It is a big job!

Work is about how we really see things. This is what *lectio* does for us: it enlivens our faith and opens our minds to the wisdom of Saint Benedict. He has that wonderful statement. I think it is one of the most beautiful statements in the Rule. He speaks about taking care of our tools. "He will regard all utensils and goods of the monastery as sacred vessels of the altar."[168] One day as a young monk, at the end of work in the garden, I observed the older monks taking a little stone and cleaning their shovel carefully—getting off the dirt and kind of shining it up. I was impressed by that. I spoke to my Father Master, and he pointed out this line in the Rule: we should take care of our tools as the vessels of the altar, as the vessels of creation.

THE MASS OF CREATION

We are celebrating the Mass of the creation. The whole of creation gives glory to God through us. As Paul says, *All are yours, and you are Christ's, and Christ is God's* (cf. 1 Cor. 3:22–23). We raised the whole of creation to a level where it can truly glorify God in a way that is worthy because we are one with Christ and can give glory to God at a divine level. Just as we assimilate food, we assimilate other things, raising them in God's glory.

We celebrate the Mass of the creation. The central moment in our life each day is when we enter into the Mass. As the Second Vatican Council said, in the Eucharist we have the summit of creation.[169] The greatest act of love that ever ascends from God in the creation is in the Mass. It is the act of Calvary. But Benedict says, We bring the whole of that up to that level of being no matter what we are doing—whatever our little or big job is in community. Or many jobs in community. Many wear several hats, God love them. There is this tremendous generosity in the community. So many people work and get things done, and help to get things done. There is a lot for which to be grateful. Whatever it is, we are celebrating this liturgy of the creation, giving glory to God.

Work is a wonderful part of our lives, but it is the *lectio* which is the time of encountering Christ and God as we allow God to speak to us through the revealed word. The wisdom of our blessed father Saint Benedict in the Rule and the wisdom of the church fathers keeps us at this level of consciousness. Work becomes a joy and an empowering moment of love that gives glory to God. So it all comes together. Not only in chapter forty-eight, but in the whole of the Rule, Saint Benedict weaves it together.

We are called to be disciples of perhaps one of the wisest men that has ever lived, Saint Benedict. It is no mere accident that millions, literally millions, through the centuries have chosen his Rule as the guide for life. There is a tremendous wisdom where he integrates it all. We go to the Rule again and again and ask him to lead us and show us how to live the Gospels in a way that brings tremendous joy and meaning to every aspect of our lives.

Let us celebrate that we are disciples of Benedict and are being guided in the way of the Gospel that leads us into the fullness of the passion, death, and resurrection of Christ. Let us be true agents of that for the whole human family, for the whole of creation.

MAY THE DIVINE ASSISTANCE REMAIN WITH US ALWAYS AMEN

XV ❧ ALL OF LIFE SHOULD BE A LENT

[14]*During the days of Lent, they should be free in the morning to read until the third hour, after which they will work at their assigned tasks until the end of the tenth hour.* [15]*During this time of Lent each one is to receive a book from the library, and is to read the whole of it straight through.* [16]*These books are to be distributed at the beginning of Lent.* [17]*Above all, one or two seniors must surely be deputed to make the rounds of the monastery while the brothers are reading.* [18]*Their duty is to see that no brother is so apathetic as to waste time or engage in idle talk to the neglect of his reading, and so not only harm himself but also distract others.* [19]*If such a monk is found—God forbid—he should be reproved a first and a second time.* [20]*If he does not amend, he must be subjected to the punishment of the rule as a warning to others.* [21]*Further, brothers ought not to associate with one another at inappropriate times.* [22]*On Sunday all are to be engaged in reading except those who have been assigned various duties.* [23]*If anyone is so remiss and indolent that he is unwilling*

or unable to study or to read, he is to be given some work in order that he may not be idle.

[1]The life of a monk ought to be a continuous Lent.

—Chapters 48 and 49
THE RULE OF SAINT BENEDICT

Brothers making their rounds is not something we observe today. The older brethren, however, might remember doing Lenten reading in common. At Lantao [near Hong Kong], we read our Lenten reading together in the chapter room from 6:45 to 7:30 PM.[170] At Spencer [Saint Joseph's Abbey in Massachusetts], we could do it at different places: the cloister, chapter house, library, or scriptorium.[171] Two brothers would be appointed to roam around. I guess the main thing was to see if the monks would stay awake.

What struck me, as I was thinking about chapter forty-eight of the Rule, was that here we are in what you might say was the golden age of monastic life—the time of the great Abbot Benedict and his community. Obviously they had some problems with people gossiping and talking when they should not have been. So we should not be too surprised to find this in our own monastic communities today. We are all a bunch of poor, weak, stupid sinners struggling along, and God is not finished with any of us yet.

The important thing, and it is what Benedict warns us about, is the monastic vice of *acedia*. *Apathetic* is the word in English, but the Latin word is *acediosus*.[172] The monk has lost the zeal that is looked for in the new man coming to the monastery.[173] The man truly seeks God and lives out that seeking of God with zeal for the work of God, zeal for being a man of obedience; and, the man has zeal when he embraces the humble way of life. Zeal gives energy to the life.

The challenge here is in living the balance that Benedict brings to monastic life. This balance is why the Rule has worked for hundreds of years. Remember the balance of keeping alive the ideal, but lovingly embracing the real. It is working practically to bring forth the fullness of the ideal. Benedict is very practical. He fully accepts that in his community are different kinds of weaknesses. Yet, he has the ideal there, too, with practical ways to move forward. We need to keep the ideal clear in our own life—as an individual and as community. That is the purpose of our *lectio*. Also, the ideal is kept clear through fraternal example and the encouragement given to each other.

We are the greatest thing in creation. We are the very image of God called into being. Even in this life—in transfiguring Taboric moments—we can experience the fullness of sharing in the divine life and joy.[174] But we are being led to the ultimate fullness of that sharing in eternal life. We are moving towards that eternal joy. While our life is being filled with the joy of the divine life, at the same time we are the poor, weak, stupid sinners who need to struggle practically with ourselves and community. This is why we have community guidelines—to support us as a community as we walk towards this divine life and support each other.

To keep in balance the ideal with the real is a real challenge of the life. If we give up the ideal, then that is acedia, and life goes nowhere. Then, we would just settle down in the real mess that we are. If we do not really accept the real and cling to some ideal, then we are being unrealistic and will burn out quickly. It is a question of keeping the ideal fully alive as individuals and as community, but at the same time lovingly embracing the real in ourselves and in our brethren and lovingly move together to the fullness of eternal joy.

THE MEANING OF HAPPINESS

As I have often said, happiness consists in knowing what you want, and then knowing you have it, or you are on the way to getting it. What we want is God. Our hearts will not rest until they rest in you, O Lord.[175] Our minds seek infinite truth. Our hearts are made for infinite love. The purpose of the structures of our life—of going apart from the world in silence in solitude—is so that we can keep alive, at that level of knowing, who we are and what we really want. Through contemplative prayer and spiritual experiences, we then know that, to some extent, we have it now or are on the way of getting it. This is the meaning of Cistercian life: we are on the way. We have committed ourselves. It is the life of the "stricter observance" in the sense that we are really committed to be in quest of the fullness of divine life and joy. That is why our life can be tremendously happy. There is a deep joy. We know what we want, and we know, to some extent, that we already enjoy it but there is infinitely more in eternal life. We are on the way to it.

When we see the failures, weaknesses, and the sins in ourselves and in our brothers, we should not let this lead to acedia. We should not let this undercut our clinging to the great call that we have to the fullness of divine life and joy. We should just humbly accept that and know that God isn't finished with us yet. Together with the Lord I can do all things in him who strengthens me (Phil. 4:13). We are on the way. That is the excitement. That is the joy of the life.

Benedict says the whole of life should be a Lent, but Lent is a time when especially we live in this joy because we have those Tabor moments—moments of transfiguration. Together with the resurrection of Lazarus, these moments are pointing to where this all leads.[176] To what?

The risen life. To the life beyond Calvary, beyond Jerusalem, to the empty tomb, to the fullness of life. That is what we are called to. To desire anything less than that is to betray ourselves—who we are, what we are made for, and the meaning of our being. To live in the joy of this promise of the risen life is the source of a deep, profound joy even as we struggle with the poor, weak, stupid things that happen all of the time. We know that these are just steps on the journey. We are on the way into the fullness.

BAPTIZED INTO CHRIST

To really get what is going on in the holy season of Lent, I think you have to get back to the basics. We have been baptized into Christ. As Paul puts it, *It is now no longer I that live, but Christ lives in me* (cf. Gal. 2:20). We are no longer simply human persons but, in some way, have been raised up to participate in the divine life (2 Pet. 1:4). As the old catechism used to say, we have been made partakers of the divine nature and life.[177]

We have been brought into a oneness with Christ that is really beyond anything we can comprehend. Jesus prayed at the Last Supper, *That all may be one, even as thou, Father, in me and I in thee; that they also may be one in us* (cf. Jn. 17:21). We know that the Father and the Son are absolutely one, even remaining distinct persons so they can truly love each other. The Father pours himself out totally to the Son in love, and the Son responds to the totality of his being in love, and that love is the Holy Spirit. They are one in that love. So, too, we have been made one with Christ in a oneness beyond anything we can comprehend. Yet, we remain distinct persons so that we and Christ may, indeed, love each other. With that love is Holy Spirit.

As Paul put it, *You have received a spirit of adoption as sons, by virtue of which we cry, "Abba! Father!"* (cf. Rom. 8:15). We have received the Holy Spirit as our spirit, because that is the reality, this is who we really are—sons of God. Then we most truly live our life as we live it with Christ, in Christ, in the sacramental mystery of the liturgy.

JESUS' PRESENCE IN THE LITURGY

Christ, in time, relives the mystery of his incarnation, presence, and salvific mission each year in the unfolding of the sacrament of the liturgy. The sacrament is not just an outward sign, it is an inner reality. What is once and forever in the eternal now of God unfolds again and again in our time, accomplishing that salvation—that mission of love—in this world.

In each of us is Christ making the redemption present in the world today. Paul puts it, *And what is lacking of the sufferings of Christ I fill up in my flesh for his body, which is the Church* (cf. Col. 1:24). In one sense, there is absolutely nothing wanting in the passion of Christ. Here is divine love expressing itself. But what is wanting is the actual temporal presence in our historical unfolding. That is made present by our living it. That is what we live in living a liturgical life. And Lent is a very special time of that. It is an intensification of entering into the Christ-mystery and living it day by day through letting the Word come alive in us. We are living that Word as we move forward to the fullness that comes in Holy Week when we live with Christ from minute to minute, from hour to hour, the culminating mystery of his life.

THE TOTAL LOVE OF CHRIST

Every moment of Christ's life here on earth was redemptive because every moment was this total love. *I do always the things that are pleasing to him* (cf. Jn. 8:29). Every moment he was a complete *yes* to the Father. It was a fullness of love; it was redemptive. At the same time, he tells us, *Greater love than this no one has, that one lay down his life for his friends* (cf. Jn. 15:13). He wanted to give that supreme, ultimate sign. So he walked on with his face set toward Jerusalem until finally he was able to get home to us how much he loves us. He went all the way to Calvary. That is the love with which we are loved, and it is the love which we are called to live. Only when we really get hold of this does our life have its tremendous meaning. All the details of our life have tremendous meaning because it is Christ—the Christ that we are—doing the things that please the Father, and in that we are bringing redemption to the world today and tomorrow.

This year we are especially blessed in having a solemn profession at Eastertime. Solemn profession is the ultimate sign for us [as monks]. We totally give ourselves over to God. In a very radical way, we die to this world. We are no longer able to possess; no longer able to give ourselves in matrimony. We totally commit ourselves to say *yes* to God in the solemn vow of obedience. In some Benedictine communities, they try to bring this out a little bit more in a sacramental sign. At the solemn profession, when the monk prostrates, they get out the funeral pall and spread it over him as though they were covering a coffin. They put the candles alongside. This man has died to the world, so that he may rise and live with Christ. We are stripped of the old man and we put on the garment of salvation—the white cowl, the beautiful robe of the resurrection.

Solemn profession is the ultimate moment of total love for God. It is the living out of that in the everyday details of life that gives those details infinite meaning. This is the reason for the structure of our monastic life—of going apart, enclosure, cloister, silence, and solitariness—to open the space for us to enter and realize, in a profoundly meaningful way, the reality that we are

Christ here and now to the Father. We are both bringing the whole of creation to the Father and bringing the redemption to the human family. It is a wondrous mystery that is far beyond us. We struggle, I certainly struggle, to live at this level of consciousness. Yet, when we do, it is wondrous.

Everything we do has so much meaning, just as the everyday, ordinary things of Christ's life: working in the carpenter shop at Nazareth, eating and washing, and going to the synagogue and singing the psalms. All that he did was saving the world. It was such a selfless love. God could have said, as he said to Moses, "Let me just wipe them out and we will start again. I will make you a father of a whole new people." Moses, in that wondrous selfless love, said, "No, no, no! Don't do that. Let me suffer for them. Let me do something for them. Don't do that" (cf. Ex. 32:10–14). Instead of wiping out the sinners, God comes to us in his tremendous love. He gives himself so completely in love to us. We are called to do the same.

The selfless gift of love that we give each day in getting up and going to choir, singing the psalms, praying, meditating, reading, and doing our jobs—why do all of this? We believe that because we have been Christ-ed, in doing this, it is Christ in us who is giving infinite glory to the Father and bringing down upon the human family the graces of redemption. We are bringing salvation to the human family. It's a mystery, but a reality.

We are tempted, though, not to even make the effort to stay with the reality. We write it off as some pious thoughts. But as both Peter and Paul told us, everything that was written in the Scriptures was written for our instruction (Rom. 15:4; 2 Pet. 1:20–21). It was to enable us to know what we could in no other way know of God's tremendous love—the power of that love and the meaning of that love in our lives. It is precisely this revelation upon which we ground our whole being: *It is now no longer I that live, but Christ lives in me* (cf. Gal. 2:20). I have been baptized into Christ. I am Christ to the world today, called upon to live my life just as Jesus did in order to bring salvation and redemption to every man, woman, and child. This is the wonder of our vocation.

JOY IN OUR LENT

Saint Benedict says our whole life should be Lent.[178] Enter more deeply into the mystery of Who am I? Who are we? We have been formed into this cell in the body of Christ. What's our meaning in the whole plan of the creation? What's our meaning in the world today? When, by the grace of the Holy Spirit and the gifts of the Holy Spirit, we come to really understand this, we begin to realize that life is tremendously meaningful. Out of that comes an intense joy, even though we may feel tired, headachy, and overburdened at having too many things to take care of. I look at my desk, and I want to run out of the room and keep on running! Lord, preserve me. There are so many things that pile up there. It is by just taking care of those little things and doing what needs to be done now.

Because I am one with Christ, my life has the power and the grace to save you and bring redemption. It is a call to a great, selfless love. I do not know the people whom I am saving in and through Christ in this mission, this obedience, this service, and this prayer, but I know that God loves them. God loves them enough to make them and keep them every moment into being. God wants to share with them the fullness of his joy. Jesus prayed at the Last Supper, *that they may have my joy made full in themselves* (cf. Jn. 17:13). That is what God wants for each one of us: complete joy. Absolute, complete joy. It is because we love him and have been brought into this oneness with him that, then, we want to do what we can—what we are called to—to fill up what is wanting in his passion (cf. Col. 1:24). To make his love present in the world and bring salvation and joy to men and women and children whom we shall only some day celebrate with in heaven.

By the grace of the Holy Spirit, the more we seek, the more we can know. We heard in today's Gospel, *Seek, and you shall find* (cf. Mt. 7:7–8). The more we seek to really understand—to find our true selves—the more we can be filled with an intense joy in the full meaningfulness of who we are. The wonder of the human person is already amazing. We are made in the image of God, called to the likeness of God. We have been taken beyond that in baptism and made true sharers in the divine life. We have been divinized. It is a wonder beyond anything we can fully grasp, but we can enter into it little by little.

The Holy Spirit can bring those moments of enlightenment and joy, and then life is so meaningful. Though it may seem like little things going on in our daily life, this is the stuff whereby God is here-and-now bringing this creation to its fullness and bringing us to the fullness of the divine joy. We enter the inner life of the Trinity and be to the Father in the Son this amazing love in the Spirit. It takes a lot of grace, fidelity, and perseverance to move into this mystery.

Following God's Illumination

God, of course, could illuminate us in an instant. There are those moments of light, and they are wonderful. But most of the time it happens little by little. As we seek, we find. I was so impressed by a lesson taught to me in India. When a man becomes a *Brahmachari*, which is something equivalent to our novices, he receives a white habit. But then, he begins a process where, if not each day, still fairly regularly, he works on dyeing his habit. When he washes it, he always puts it into a yellow dye. Little by little the habit takes on a deep yellow color until it becomes almost like a flame. It is a sign of how he is to be transformed by the divine light and become a light.

It is striking to find the same images in the different traditions. One day I was with an ecumenical group and we went to visit Nicholas Arseniev (d. 1977), one of the great spiritual fathers of the Orthodox tradition at St. Vladimir's Theological Seminary. He was talking to us about entering more and more into the divine light and letting the light enter more and more into us. Suddenly, he rose up. He almost glowed and he said, "Until we become like fire and the flames shoot forth from every one of our fingers. . . ." It was like a saying from the Desert Fathers. He himself was transformed with light at that moment.

We are to let the Light who is Christ come alive in us so that we are a light to the world. As the monastery is a city set on the mountain, we as individuals are the candle on the candlestick. Each of us is giving our light. It is not an easy thing to live at a level of such consciousness or even to consistently and faithfully seek that consciousness. I know that from my own life experience. But that is where community is such a help. The arrangement of the life, prayers and *lectio* and all these things, remind us and urge us on, calling us forth. We fail and fail again, perhaps more than we should, but the community life keeps us going.

THE MEANING OF LENT

The meaning of Lent is a time when we really stop and ask ourselves, What is the meaning of it all? Who am I? What are we called to? It is a time to ask the deep questions and begin to live in those deep questions and come to know the joy of life's meaningfulness. I'm sure that we each find a part of ourselves that does not want to ask the questions because the more we realize life's meaning, the more we have to live as a light for the world. There are little parts of us that want to hang onto this, that, and the other thing—our own little practices that somewhat clutter up our lives. We do not want to let everything go and become pure light, pure fire. But we have to have the humility to at least seek. To try to do the little things. To try to be with the awareness of the moment. To use the Lenten readings, the Offices, the prayers, and the example of each other to take the next little step. Then we can be sure that if we do, we shall find. We shall see our Lord Jesus as he is, and we shall be like him—this pure love, pure joy, and radiance.

What Lent invites us to is quite fantastic. *Eye has not seen or ear heard, nor has it entered into the heart of man, what things God has prepared for those who love him* (cf. 1 Cor. 2:9; Isa. 64:3). Holy Spirit makes it known to us. We have a great dependence on the Spirit. Come Holy Spirit, enlighten us, encourage us, strengthen us, illuminate us, bring us into the reality. Give us the courage, the gift of fortitude to go on. The gift of knowledge and the gift of understanding. Without him, we can do nothing (Jn. 15:5). With him, all things are possible (Phil. 4:13). Let us cry out. Let us seek. Let us hope. Let us pray. Let us enter into Lent as fully as we possibly can.

Let us, with great compassion, embrace our own weaknesses and struggles, and those of our brothers. But let us keep clear in our life what we are called to. Let us concretely and realistically move toward that as we encourage and support each other. Then we will come together to the fullness of Easter and eternal life.

MAY THE DIVINE ASSISTANCE
REMAIN WITH US ALWAYS AMEN

XVI • THE BURIAL OF ALLELUIA

¹*The life of a monk ought to be a continuous Lent.* ²*Since few, however, have the strength for this, we urge the entire community during these days of Lent to keep its manner of life most pure* ³*and to wash away in this holy season the negligences of other times.* ⁴*This we can do in a fitting manner by refusing to indulge evil habits and by devoting ourselves to prayer with tears, to reading, to compunction of heart and self-denial.* ⁵*During these days, therefore, we will add to the usual measure of our service something by way of private prayer and abstinence from food or drink,* ⁶*so that each of us will have something above the assigned measure to offer God of his own will with the joy of the Holy Spirit (1 Thess. 1:6).* ⁷*In other words, let each one deny himself some food, drink, sleep, needless talking and idle jesting, and look forward to holy Easter with joy and spiritual longing.* ⁸*Everyone should, however, make known to the abbot what he intends to do, since it ought to be done with his prayer and approval.* ⁹*Whatever is undertaken*

without the permission of the spiritual father will be reckoned as presumption and vainglory, not deserving a reward. [10]Therefore, everything must be done with the abbot's approval.

—Chapter 49
THE RULE OF SAINT BENEDICT

Saint Benedict touches on Lent again and again in the Rule, especially when he is talking about the Divine Office. One chapter very curiously talks about the times of saying alleluia.

From the holy feast of Easter until Pentecost, "alleluia" is always said with both the psalms and the responsorials. Every night from Pentecost until the beginning of Lent, it is said only with the last six psalms of Vigils. Vigils, Lauds, Prime, Terce, Sext and None are said with "alleluia" every Sunday except in Lent; at Vespers, however, a refrain is used. "Alleluia" is never said with responsorials except from Easter to Pentecost.[179]

The Medieval monks had a liturgy for this little provision for alleluia. At Vespers, on the eve of the first Sunday of Lent, they would have solemn burial of alleluia. They would put alleluia in a coffin and solemnly carry alleluia off to the cemetery or the crypt for burial until alleluia arose with Christ at Easter.

Benedict makes many provisions for Lent in the Rule, but chapter forty-nine is devoted to the observance of Lent. He speaks of monks undertaking particular observances to mark Lent for themselves. What is the purpose? It is that we have the joy of spiritual longing. Lent is really a time of freeing ourselves and opening ourselves more and more to the fullness of Easter.

What is the thing that really gives your life push— meaning and satisfaction? What are you really longing for from the deep depths of your heart? What do you really want? We can say, God, union with God, happiness, peace, friendship, and intimacy. But to really get down to it: what is the thing that we really want? That is what Benedict is talking about here. To really get in touch with what we are longing for.

Benedict sees Lent as fully entering into the Paschal mystery. It is a dying to the false self, dying to all our sins. It is dying to all the junk and nonsense that fill our lives and living to the reality of who we are as men who have been baptized into Christ. We are men called to share the fullness of the divine joy—the divine life. That is why God made us. Through baptism, God has brought us to that level of being able to share the fullness of divine life.

Benedict says at the beginning: "The life of a monk ought to be a continuous Lent. Since few, however, have the strength for this, we urge the entire community during these days of Lent to keep its manner of life most pure."[180] And he comes up with the idea of doing some particular little thing that is sort of a hook on which everything hangs. Each day, do some little thing that says this is a special time. It is a time that we are keeping before us to find out what we really want, what our deepest being is crying out for. It is a time to cut through some of the stuff which we have been grabbing at to try to find some fulfillment, some happiness, some meaning. We realize that any and all has its meaning only to the extent that it is a means of coming to what we really want and what we are really made for.

PURITY OF HEART

Lent is a time of coming to purity of heart. It is the pure of heart who see God. It is a challenge, but the community supports us by certain signs, symbols, and actions. The older monks may remember how dramatic Lent once was. We used to put up a great Lenten curtain in the church. Each time you entered the church, you were confronted with this mass of purple that said this is a special time. You would be getting ready to penetrate through the veil and come to the fullness of the Paschal joy. You couldn't miss Lent. It just knocked you over. We had a lot of other things, too. We had much more fasting with days of bread of water. We had penitential processions through the cloister as we sang the penitential psalms. Then we would prostrate in church and chant the litany of saints. There were a lot of things that constantly reminded us of the special time of Lent. What can we do today, and what do we want to do as a community to support each member of the community in entering more fully into the full meaning of this wonderful time?

LECTIO DURING LENT

In chapter forty-eight, Benedict sets forth an observance which is still prevalent in our order. He is talking in that chapter of the daily manual labor, but he goes on to say:

> During the days of Lent, they should be free in the morning to read until the third hour, after which they will work at their assigned tasks until the end of the tenth hour. During this time of Lent each one is to receive a book from the library, and is to read the whole of it straight through. These books are to be distributed at the beginning of Lent.[181]

Benedict is speaking of *lectio*, which consists of *lectio* (reading), *meditatio* (reflection), *oratio* (response), and *cotemplatio* (rest).[182] The idea was that you began your prayer by letting the Lord have the first word. For monks back then, *lectio* did not always mean reading a book in the sense that today we can easily pick up a book. They did not have books and very few even knew how to read. In most monasteries, though, choir monks were taught to read. *Lectio* in Benedict's time was calling up to memory what was previously memorized.

Older monks will remember spending most of their postulancy memorizing psalms and prayers. We memorized the Little Office of the Blessed Virgin. And we carried a lot of the Scriptures in our head. In Benedict's time, even more memorization was being done. *Lectio* was a time when you sat down and let the Lord speak to you. You then responded to that and moved into contemplation.

During Lent, Benedict provided extra time for reading as well as a special book to be read. He said, "During this time of Lent each one is to receive a book from the library, and is to read the whole of it straight through." A special word from the Lord was to be heard during Lent.

When I was a young religious, you had no say about the book. You were just given a book. On the first Sunday of Lent, you would be thinking, What am I going to have to read for the next forty days? For both my first and second year novitiate, I was presented with Saint Alphonsus Liguori's *The Glories of the Blessed Virgin Mary*. In recent times, for the monasteries who still have the distribution of books, each monk usually chooses the book himself or talks it over with his spiritual guide. Spending significant time with that particular book and that particular author helps in the entering into the Paschal mystery.

Benedict, because he was a very practical man, goes on to say:

Above all, one or two seniors must surely be deputed to make the rounds of the monastery while the brothers are reading. Their duty is to see that no brother is so apathetic as to waste time or engage in idle talk to the neglect of his reading, and so not only harm himself but also distract others. If such a monk is found—God forbid—he should be reproved a first and a second time. If he does not amend, he must be subjected to the punishment of the rule as a warning to others. Further, brothers ought not to associate with one another at inappropriate times.[183]

Benedict also speaks about Sunday as being a day for *lectio*.[184]

As we look at Lent as individuals and as community, it is a time for renewal in *lectio*. It is a time for opening ourselves in a renewed and special way to letting the Lord open up our lives in relationship with him through *lectio*.

We allow his word to be heard and resound, and then respond to it after giving it ample time.

True friendship only grows when friends give each other time. The Lord wants us to be his friends in a most deep and intimate and total way. We enter into the divine relationship with the realization that this relationship occurs in our lives in human ways. One of them is spending time with a friend. *Lectio* is precisely that. We sit down, and we know the Lord is present in his Word. We sit down and let him speak to us, and we speak to him. We spend that time with him, which opens out into real contemplation. The Holy Spirit brings us into deep communion with God with the gifts of wisdom, understanding, and knowledge.

What do we as a community want to do to support each member of the community in living the Lenten mystery in fullness? Let us come together to one of the greatest Easters of our lives. May each of us fully experience, and we as a community experience, the fact that we have been baptized into Christ and have risen with Christ. We are even now called to live the risen life.

MAY THE DIVINE ASSISTANCE AMEN
REMAIN WITH US ALWAYS

XVII · JOY IN THE HOLY SPIRIT

⁵During these days, therefore, we will add to the usual measure of our service something by way of private prayer and abstinence from food or drink, ⁶so that each of us will have something above the assigned measure to offer God of his own will with the joy of the Holy Spirit (1 Thess. 1:6). ⁷In other words, let each one deny himself some food, drink, sleep, needless talking and idle jesting, and look forward to holy Easter with joy and spiritual longing.

—Chapter 49
THE RULE OF SAINT BENEDICT

In the midst of Lent, it is good to stop and look around. As I listen to the words of Benedict, I ask myself, To what extent during these days have I been living in the joy of the Holy Spirit, looking eagerly forward to Easter? To what extent have I been keeping up to my Lenten practices in prayer and self denial?

This man Benedict fascinates me with his emphasis on joy. How many people have you run into in your life who, when you speak of Lent, the first thing that comes to mind is joy? Where is this man coming from?

He has set his mark. This is what Lent is all about—entering into the fullness and joy of Easter. Everything else that you do is in the light of that. If I do more praying and fasting, it is just to look forward to, and to be aware of, the joy of the Resurrection. The power of that excitement! What I am called to as a man who has been baptized into the risen Christ is to live in the light of the Resurrection. Right now. The powerful grace of Easter calls us to enter more fully into the wonder of that joy.

If I reflect on what Lent has meant to me and it has not been marked by joy, why not? Why am I not filled with joy at the prospect of Easter? What can I do about it? What am I going to do about it? Maybe I do not want to be happy after all. Maybe I have given up all hope that I really could be happy. Maybe I want to step forward, as Paul says, forgetting what has been up to now (cf. Phil. 3:13). Set the mark which is the full joy of Easter. Then look at what I need to do—what I want to do—during the days of Lent so that Easter joy can just explode in my being.

Or, am I coming up against something in my past? "I have never been a very joyous person. This is ridiculous. I cannot be a joyous person," I might say. Is that where we are coming from? Do we want to come from there? Or can we step out?

A Sign of Hope and Joy

As the grace of Easter shines upon us more fully in Lenten days, what can we do to let it in our own lives so that it can shine through us into the community? Then it can shine forth from the community to a world that so much needs the joyful hope of resurrection. I think that is what a contemplative community is all about—to be a sign and a source of hope and joy. To be, in some way, instruments which God can use to fulfill Christ's prayer, "Father, that they may share my joy and that their joy may be complete" (cf. Jn. 15:11; 17:13).

We love Christ. Every one of us loves Christ so much that we gave our life to him. In an even more radical way than a man gives himself to his wife, we have given ourselves to Christ. So we want what Christ wants. He wants us to be filled with the joy of God—that joy that was his as the Son of God in communion with the Father and the Holy Spirit. Somehow or other, there is this profound paradox or mystery: Christ suffered as no man has ever suffered. He wept over Jerusalem. He hungered. He thirst. He labored. He was tired, disappointed, and betrayed. It was all there. Yet from the depths of his divine being, this person was filled with the divine joy. He *is* the divine joy. That's the kind of joy I think he is talking about here. Even as we have the heartaches, headaches, concerns, pains, and tears, there is a deep joy down in the depths.

CHRIST—A SOURCE OF JOY FOR OTHERS

I think that is what Benedict is talking about here when he is talking about prayer, fasting, and abstaining during Lent. In some way we are denying ourselves so we can get a little more in touch—live more out of—the profound joy that shines forth from the risen Christ. This is joy that shines into the life of each of us who has been baptized into Christ. It is the joy that shines forth from us into the world if we are transparent. The asceticism and the prayer is to help us to become more transparent so that we ourselves may experience the joy more fully and profoundly. Then we will be a hope and source of that joy for our brothers and sisters.

May we always enter Lent with renewed hope, forgetting what is behind, setting the mark, and pressing forward to the fullness of life in the risen Jesus.

MAY THE DIVINE ASSISTANCE AMEN
REMAIN WITH US ALWAYS

XVIII ❧ INCLINE THE
EAR OF YOUR HEART

¹Do not grant newcomers to the monastic life an easy entry, ²but, as the Apostle says, Test the spirits to see if they are from God *(1 Jn. 4:1). ³Therefore, if someone comes and keeps knocking at the door, and if at the end of four or five days he has shown himself patient in bearing his harsh treatment and difficulty of entry, and has persisted in his request, ⁴then he should be allowed to enter and stay in the guest quarters for a few days. ⁵After that, he should live in the novitiate, where the novices study, eat and sleep. ⁶A senior chosen for his skill in winning souls should be appointed to look after them with careful attention. ⁷The concern must be whether the novice truly seeks God and whether he shows eagerness for the Work of God, for obedience and for trials. ⁸The novice should be clearly told all the hardships and difficulties that will lead him to God.*

—Chapter 58
THE RULE OF SAINT BENEDICT

[EDITOR'S NOTE: The following talk was given on the
occasion of the clothing of a novice by the abbot. The
ceremony, which signifies the official beginning of the
canonical novitiate, takes place in the presence of the
community. At this point in his journey, the person
wishing to enter the novitiate has discerned his
monastic vocation with the vocation director and
novice master of the monastery. Coming before the
abbot, he expresses his desire to enter the novitiate (a
two-and-a-half-year period of study of the Cistercian
monastic traditions and charisms). The ceremony
begins with the person wishing to be received as a
novice entering the chapter room, prostrating before
the abbot, and verbally making his request to be
received as a novice. He then rises and listens to a
reading from chapter fifty-eight ("The Procedure for
Receiving Brothers") of the Rule of Saint Benedict.
The abbot gives words of encouragement and then
clothes the novice in a novice habit.]

Saint Benedict goes on in chapter fifty-eight to say that
the Holy Rule is to be read to the novice three times.
Benedict provided that after two months, the Rule be read
straight through. After six more months have passed, the
Rule is read again. After another four months, the Rule is

read for the third time. Then, at the end of the year, the novice makes a petition and is consecrated a monk. In our day, however, we do not move so quickly.

Saint Benedict stressed that the man entering the monastic life be told forthrightly—even bluntly—of the hardships and difficulties that will lead him to God.[185] Also, let him be told—through listening and reading— about this Rule which he is choosing to serve. If you can keep it, come. If not, you are free to leave.[186] It is a process of entering into this wisdom of Saint Benedict. Our hearts and minds are formed so that the Rule becomes the way to follow Christ the Lord.

Being Formed through Listening

It has been said that our father Saint Bernard knew the Bible by heart. I do not know how true that is, but he was certainly filled with the Bible. Benedict is that way, too. And you will be, too, if you keep going to the Office, pray the psalms, listen to readings, and doing the *lectio* [spiritual reading]. You become so filled with the Scripture that you almost have to express yourself in a scriptural way.

When reciting the Hebrew poetry in the psalms, we come across an idea put forth in one way, followed by the same idea presented in another way using images. This structure brings us to a fuller understanding, experience, and comprehension of the psalms. We find this at the beginning of the Rule, too. Saint Benedict says, "Listen, son, to the precepts of the master. Incline the ear of your heart."[187] "Listen, son" is followed by an image, "incline the ear of your heart." *Et inclina aurem cordis tui.* It is the image of someone straining to hear everything. You get your ear out there. You want to receive every word being said. You want to get the fullness of it. So the idea is to incline the ear of your heart. It is of the heart, not just the mind; it is the whole man. Benedict is saying that this listening is an attitude where you are all there. There is a desire to receive the Rule fully. It is a zeal for listening to the Holy Rule—its teaching and wisdom.

As we just heard in chapter fifty-eight of the Rule about receiving our brethren, Benedict says to see if the newcomer truly seeks God. The signs for that are in three zeals. Zeal is defined as *eagerness* in this text of the RB 1980. The Latin *sollicitus* means "zeal." Zeal for the work of God, zeal for obedience, and zeal for the humble way of life.

Zeal for the work of God means not just coming to Office and being there all of the time. It is being there fully through your singing, listening, and responding. Even more deeply, as Saint Benedict says in the nineteenth chapter ("The Discipline of the Psalmody"), you bring the mind into harmony with the heart—the spirit with the voice.[188] We allow the ideas and words to form and shape us, and to make them truly our own.

The same is true of obedience. It is not just doing what we are told. Benedict, in the fourth step of humility, says that we are to embrace and endure everything not only without murmuring but with joy. This way of humility, found in chapter seven of the Rule, is the heart of his spiritual teaching.

That in this obedience under difficult, unfavorable, or even unjust conditions, his heart quietly embraces suffering and endures it without weakening or seeking escape. For Scripture has it: *Anyone who perseveres to the end will be saved* (Mt. 10:22), and again, *Be brave of heart and rely on the LORD* (Ps. 27:14). Another passage shows how the faithful must endure everything, even contradiction, for the Lord's sake, saying in the person of those who suffer, *For your sake we are put to death continually; we are regarded as sheep marked for slaughter* (Rom. 8:36; Ps. 44:22). They are so confident in their expectation of reward from God that they continue joyfully. . . .[189]

Even in the zeal for these contradictions of life, you not only embrace them without murmuring, but embrace them with joy. It is with that same kind of wholeheartedness and zeal which one "inclines the ear of the heart" in the reading of the wisdom of Saint Benedict in his Rule. It is to seek and receive into your whole being the wisdom of the Rule.

This is what led Saint Robert of Molesme, our founder, through his whole life. In founding the Cistercian Order at Cîteaux, he was seeking the opportunity to really live the Rule, to be fully formed and shaped by it. We mentioned earlier about Saint Robert of Fountains, who led the monks from York to Fountains. With both Roberts, there was this desire to live fully the wisdom of the Rule. And it is our desire. On Wednesday we celebrate the founding of our monastery when the monks came from Gethsemani Abbey [in Kentucky] to [found Our Lady of the Holy Spirit Monastery in] Georgia. They came to fully live the Holy Rule in Georgia just as they had at Gethsemani. We are all challenged to ask ourselves, Is this zeal alive in us today? This is what the Lord calls you to as you walk in the way and embrace the way of the Rule. We are not eager for the Rule in itself. We are eager for the Rule as an expression of the Gospels. We are eager to live the Gospels because we want union with Christ. As Benedict puts it in the Rule, prefer absolutely nothing to the love of Christ.[190]

My first spiritual father used to say to me, "God is where his will is." We want to know the will of God so we can embrace it fully and be in complete union and harmony with Christ who sought always to do the things that please the Father (Jn. 8:29). We embrace God's will because of our love for Jesus Christ. You enter into the way of the Rule today. It is a wonderful way, a traditional way, and a proven way of coming into harmony with the whole of Christ.

[EDITOR'S NOTE: At this point in the talk, Abbot Basil turned to the man seeking to become a novice.]

And so, I ask you, brother, are you willing to enter into this way of Saint Benedict, the Gospels, and the communion of Christ?

MAY THE DIVINE ASSISTANCE REMAIN WITH US ALWAYS. AMEN

XIX • THE GOOD ZEAL OF MONKS

¹Just as there is a wicked zeal of bitterness which separates from God and leads to hell, ²so there is a good zeal which separates from evil and leads to God and everlasting life. ³This, then, is the good zeal which monks must foster with fervent love: ⁴They should each try to be the first to show respect to the other (Rom. 12:10), *⁵supporting with the greatest patience one another's weaknesses of body or behavior, ⁶and earnestly competing in obedience to one another.* ⁷No one is to pursue what he judges better for himself, but instead, what he judges better for someone else. *⁸To their fellow monks they show the pure love of brothers; ⁹to God, loving fear; ¹⁰to their abbot, unfeigned and humble love. ¹¹Let them prefer nothing whatever to Christ, ¹²and may he bring us all together to everlasting life.*

—Chapter 72
THE RULE OF SAINT BENEDICT

I would like to share this evening on what is the crowning chapter of our Holy Rule, chapter seventy-two ("The

Good Zeal of Monks"). The last chapter of the Rule, chapter seventy-three ("This Rule [Is] Only a Beginning of Perfection"), is really an epilogue. Benedict writes that he has just written this little rule for beginners, and you can find a fuller teaching in Basil, Cassian, the church fathers, and, of course, in the Scriptures. Chapter seventy-two, however, is the crowning chapter of this Rule.

Benedict depended a great deal on the *Rule of the Master*. In fact, there are those who believe that Benedict is actually the Master, and the *Rule of the Master* was the first rule he wrote when he was superior of the twelve monasteries at Subiaco. For the most part, the Holy Rule depends on the *Rule of the Master*. But as we listen to the *Rule of the Master*, as we have been at Sext, we can say thanks be to God that Benedict moved on from there.[191] Whether he wrote that Rule or used that Rule, Benedict went on at Monte Cassino to write his own rule for monasteries.

We know, too, that in the last part of the Rule there is a collection of verses which scholars believe are not really drawing on the *Rule of the Master*. They seem to draw more from Saint Augustine. Saint Augustine did not actually write a rule, although it is spoken of as the Rule of Saint Augustine.[192] It is the guidance he wrote for the canons of his cathedral. The last chapters of the Holy Rule of Saint Benedict are influenced by Saint Augustine. Augustine had a tremendous influence on our Cistercian fathers. Saint Bernard uses Augustine a great deal, and Saint Aelred of Rievaulx had Augustine's *Confessions* on his bed table.

In this crowning chapter, chapter seventy-two, Benedict speaks of the good zeal of monks. He liked that word *zeal*. It is a powerful word that is used in the Scriptures. And there is something about Benedict that is zealous. There is a certain energy to him, a certain vibrancy and vitality. He uses *hasten* (*curritur*, *festinat*) in his Rule several times.[193] There is an eagerness; there was a fire burning in him—the fire of the Holy Spirit.

Having good zeal are Benedict's last words to his monks. He begins by talking about a wicked zeal which "separates from God and leads to hell" and a good zeal "which separates from vice and leads to God and ever-lasting life." This is the same pattern at the beginning of the psalter. The first psalm speaks about the way of the wicked and the way of the good. *Happy those who do not follow the counsel of the wicked, nor go the way of sinners, nor sit in company with scoffers* (Ps. 1:1).

Matthew sums up the teaching of our Lord in the Sermon on the Mount when Jesus speaks about the good way and the evil way—the narrow way that leads to life and the broad way that leads to death (Mt. 7:13–14).

Benedict is saying that there is this good zeal which "separates from vice." We are all born vicious. That is

186

part of our heritage. And we have all added our own vices. Our life is seeking freedom, freedom from our vices, and freedom to be completely who we are as men formed in the image and likeness of God—as men called to be totally with God in Christ. It is this good zeal which separates us from the bonds, habits, and slavery of the vice and leads us to God and eternal life.

THE WAY OF GROWING INTO GOD

Benedict goes on to describe this. It is really a description of what he sees as a way of spirituality, a way of growth into the fullness, a way of going into God. *Hunc ergo zelum ferventissimo amore exerceant monachi.* "The monk is to make this zeal his own with a most fervent, burning love." The word he uses for love is *amore*, not *caritate*, which he will use later in the chapter. *Amore* means a natural, passionate love. A monk should enter into this way with a burning passion; his whole being should be wanting to walk in this way.

Benedict describes this idea of *amore*. He speaks of the different elements. The first one is *honore se invicem praeveniant*, and the translation of this in RB 1980 is, "*They should each try to be the first to show respect to the other* (cf. Rom. 12:10)." The Latin is to honor each other. The monk should be the first there to honor his brother, to have respect for his brother. He does not wait until the brother does something to deserve it or merit it. He is the first to honor his brother, and he *wants* to honor him.

Any kind of relationship that is going to go anywhere has to begin with respect. We respect and honor the other. Yes, we are a bunch of poor, weak, stupid sinners, but we are all on the way. God is not finished with any of us. We all have our messy spots, but we honor each other because each of us is the very image of God. Each of us is the beloved son of God. Each has been baptized into Christ— made one with the very son of God. Everyone here is a person of good zeal. Think of the privilege of living in a community like this. We live with men who are saying *yes* to the divine call.

First of all, we honor one another. Then, he goes on— very realistically—to say *infirmitates suas sive corporum sive morum patientissime tolerent*. "We tolerate, with the greatest possible patience, the infirmities of body" and of the way of *morum*—"the way of acting, functioning, the way we present ourselves, the way we live." We tolerate these. Our infirmities are not good things; they are the effects of sin. The debilities of our body and spirit are the effects of sin. They are not good things in themselves, but we tolerate them with *patientissime,* the greatest possible patience.

Benedict ends the prologue by saying, "we shall through patience share in the sufferings of Christ that we may deserve also to share in his kingdom."[194] It is through patience that we share in the passion of Christ. What do I have to be patient with? Not only my brother's infirmities but my own infirmities. *Our* infirmities. We all have these infirmities. As we get older, we have to constantly sanctify our diminishments and our weaknesses. There are the physical diminishments. We cannot hear so well. We cannot see so well. We cannot remember so well. Our knees ache. Our back aches. We have to help each other more and more along the journey. But there are also the infirmities of the spirit, *morum*. "The way we act." The different habits. The different ways that people respond to life. The different weaknesses that people have.

Sometimes it is in old age that we get a glimpse of how virtuous a person is. When they get to a point where they no longer have much control of what they have been controlling all the years, such as anger, gluttony, sloth. They are now no longer able to control them, and we see the weaknesses so clearly. But we should honor them. How wonderful it was that they lived such a virtuous life as long as they could. We honor one another, and we tolerate with the greatest patience all the weaknesses.

Benedict goes on to say, *oboedientiam sibi certatim impendant*. "We obey one another competitively." We obey one another, but *certatim. Certatim* expresses the idea of a certain jostling. If everybody is going to try to obey each other, obviously there is going to be a certain competition there. That is what Benedict is saying. You struggle to be the one who is able to obey your brother.

Benedict develops that. *Nullus quod sibi utile iudicat sequatur, sed quod magis alio.* "Nobody seeks to do what is best for himself, but he seeks rather to do what is best for his brother." He is always putting his brother first. Not what is best for me but what is best for you. It is living for others, the giving of your life for others. To love one another as I have loved you (Jn. 13:34; 15:12). And Jesus gave his whole life. For Benedict, we are to give ourselves, to be there, to do what is best for others rather than seek what is best for ourselves.

LOVE AND REVERENCE

What is this all leading to? *Caritatem fraternitatis caste impendant.* "They love each other chastely with charity, with that divinely infused love." *Fraternitatis.* "The divinely infused love of brothers." It is the realization that divine love is poured into us which is Holy Spirit. Charity is the Holy Spirit living in us. It is the love of brothers. Because we have all been made one with Christ, we are sons of the Father. We are truly brothers to each other. We love each other chastely as brothers with the divine love given to us. In this honoring each other, tolerating all the weaknesses, seeking what is best for each other, we are, indeed, loving each other with this divine love—with the love which Christ loves us. To love one another as he has loved us.

Then Benedict says, *amore Deum timeant*. "To fear God with this almost passion." Fear, here, is not servile fear; it is reverential fear. You have to begin with reverence before you can go on to love. It is this reverence for God, a passionate love for God. God is God! Be wide open to let the divine reality invade you, and your whole life is spent in adoration.

What Benedict says next is interesting; it is unexpected. You think now that after he has talked about the fear of God, he will immediately talk about the love of God. Instead, he drops in, *abbatem suum sincera et humili caritate diligant*. "Love his abbot with a sincere and humble charity." This tells us how Benedict sees the abbot. The abbot is the sacrament of Christ. He holds the place of Christ in the monastery.[195] It is through this sacrament that Christ is present to us in community. There is a oneness in community as the brothers love their abbot with a humble charity. Humble because this guy is a poor, weak sinner like everybody else. It takes a lot of humility to really love him. Benedict wants it to be a sincere love despite his weakness, despite everything else. Sincerely loving him. Why? Because he is the sacrament of Christ, and Christ is the way.

191

CHRIST IS THE WAY OF ETERNAL LIFE

Benedict immediately goes on, *Christo omnino nihil praeponant.* "Absolutely nothing is to be placed before Christ." This is the crown of it. Christ is first, center, power, and the meaning of our life—the total center. The abbot has this meaning because he is the sacrament of Christ, and we need sacraments. He is there to help us come to Christ. But absolutely nothing is to be preferred to Christ.[196]

Benedict completes this chapter with *qui nos pariter ad vitam aeternam perducat.* "It is Christ who leads us to eternal life." The good zeal he is talking about is essentially Christ who leads us to it. Benedict has that one significant word there, *pariter*: who leads us together to eternal life. We go together. Benedict is a cenobite through and through. As monks gathered together in community, we are one in Christ. Together Christ leads us to eternal life. We go together.

Benedict traces this whole way of honoring one another, caring for each other, wanting what is best for each other, loving each other with Christ's love, brotherly love. We are then able to love God, to love Christ. Loving the abbot is the sacrament by which Christ leads us, but ultimately, it is Christ who is the center. It is Christ who leads us all together into life eternal.

The beginning of that life is already here. We are already led into eternal life. We have eternal life within us. We are baptized into the risen Christ who lives now and dies no more (Rom. 6:9). And I live now, not I, but Christ lives in me (Gal. 2:20). This is, in Benedict's mind, where this way leads. It is the whole way of the Rule leading us to this fullness of life in Christ Jesus, life together, life centered totally in risen Christ. For Christ is the risen Christ in us and in our midst—in each other. Above all, we find Christ in the community and in each other.

MAY THE DIVINE ASSISTANCE AMEN
REMAIN WITH US ALWAYS

1. RB prol. 1.
2. RB prol. 1–2.
3. See Saint Bernard's commentary on the Song of Songs, sermon 27.
4. Father Henri Nouwen was ordained in Holland and trained as a psychologist and a theologian. He taught at Notre Dame University, Yale Divinity School, and for three years at Harvard. At the time of his death he was the pastor of Daybreak in Toronto, a community of L'Arche, a worldwide organization that provides homes for the mentally and physically handicapped.
5. Henri Nouwen, *The Wounded Healer* (New York: Image-Doubleday, 1972, 1979).
6. Henri Nouwen, *Return of the Prodigal Son* (New York: Image-Doubleday, 1994).
7. RB prol. 2.
8. *The Works of William of St. Thierry: On Contemplating God, Prayer, Meditations* vol. 1, trans. Sister Penelope, Cistercian Fathers Series, no. 3 (Kalamazoo, MI: Cistercian Publications, 1971), 74.
9. RB 58:7.
10. Louis J. Lekai writes about the founding of Fountains Abbey in *The Cistercians: Ideals and Reality* (Kent, OH: The Kent State University Press, 1977), 38.
11. "The Epistle of Thurstan of York" in M. Basil Pennington, *The Last of the Fathers: The Cistercian Fathers of the Twelfth Century, A Collection of Essays* (Still River, MA: St. Bede's, 1983), 22. See also M. Basil

Pennington, "Three Early Documents," *Cistercian Studies* 4, no. 2 (1969): 142–158.

12. "The Epistle of Thurstan of York," 22.

13. Ibid.

14. Ibid., 24.

15. *The Rule of Saint Benedict in English*, trans. Timothy Fry (Collegeville, MN: Liturgical Press, 1981). This edition is commonly known by scholars and monks as "RB 1980."

16. Translation from the Confraternity-Douay version of the Old Testament (Rockford, IL: Catholic Book Publishing, 1957).

17. Abbot Basil sometimes is using the translation of the Rule from the Abbey of Gethsemani (1942). It uses "precept" as a translation of the Latin *praecepta*. The RB 1980 translates *praecepta* as "instructions."

18. The Rule from the Abbey of Gethsemani has "incline the ear of your heart." In the RB 1980, it is "attend to them with the ear of your heart."

19. From the Rule (Abbey of Gethsemani, 1942). The RB 1980 translation has "attend to them with the ear of your heart."

20. This is Abbot Basil's translation. He uses "laziness" instead of "sloth," which is used by both the RB 1980 and the 1942 Abbey of Gethsemani translations.

21. Abbot Basil had a knee infection at the time.

22. RB 66:8.

23. RB prol. 1.

24. RB prol. 3.

25. For the Cistercian Order of the Strict Observance, the monastic vows are stability, fidelity to the monastic way of life, and obedience.

26. See Edith Scholl, "A Will and Two Ways: *Voluntas Propria, Voluntas Communis*," *Cistercian Studies*

Quarterly 30, no. 2 (1995): 191–203.

27. RB prol. 3.
28. RB 72:11.
29. See *On Loving God by Bernard of Clairvaux with An Analytical Commentary by Emero Stiegman*, Cistercian Fathers Series no. 13B (Kalamazoo, MI: Cistercian Publications, 1995).
30. RB prol. 4.
31. RB prol. 5.
32. RB prol. 6.
33. RB prol. 7.
34. RB prol. 6.
35. RB prol. 7.
36. RB prol. 7.
37. RB 5:1–4.
38. RB prol. 49.
39. RB 7:67. Emphasis retained.
40. RB prol. 2.
41. RB prol. 4.
42. Abbot Basil is using the RB 1980 translation.
43. RB prol. 8.
44. RB prol. 38.
45. RB prol. 8–10.
46. RB prol. 8.
47. RB prol. 9.
48. RB prol. 9.
49. RB prol. 9.
50. RB prol. 9.
51. RB prol. 10.
52. RB prol. 10.
53. RB prol. 11.

54. RB prol. 12.

55. RB prol. 13.

56. RB prol. 1.

57. RB prol. 10.

58. RB prol. 12.

59. RB prol. 13.

60. RB prol. 13.

61. RB prol. 14–18.

62. RB prol. 18.

63. RB prol. 19.

64. Reference to prol. 15.

65. RB prol. 17.

66. RB prol. 17.

67. RB prol. 18.

68. RB prol. 20–21.

69. RB prol. 21.

70. See "The Epistle of Thurstan of York," in M. Basil Pennington, *The Last of the Fathers: The Cistercian Fathers of the Twelfth Century, a Collection of Essays* (Still River, MA: St. Bede's, 1983), 21–32. See also M. Basil Pennington, "Three Early Documents," *Cistercian Studies* 4, no. 2 (1969): 142–58.

71. RB prol. 21.

72. Abbot Basil attended the Cathedral College of the Immaculate Conception in Brooklyn, New York, from 1945 to 1950. He entered Saint Joseph's Abbey at Spencer, Massachusetts, on June 18, 1951.

73. RB prol. 9.

74. RB prol. 15.

75. RB prol. 23.

76. RB prol. 15–17.

77. In 1979, Pope John Paul II asked the Pontifical Academy of Sciences to study the celebrated and controversial "Galileo case." A papal commission of scholars was established in 1981. On October 31, they presented their finding that Galileo's judges, erroneously believing that the Copernican theory conflicted with revealed truth, wrongfully forbade Galileo to teach the theory.

78. See M. Basil Pennington, *Poetry as Prayer: The Psalms* (Boston: Pauline Books & Media, 2001).

79. From "The Highwayman," a poem by Alfred Noyes (1880–1958).

80. RB prol. 17.

81. Quotations of Psalm 1 taken from the Confraternity-Douay version (Rockford, IL: Catholic Book Publishing, 1957).

82. RB prol. 17.

83. RB prol. 4.

84. Old Testament references to an unblemished lamb include Leviticus 23:12; Exodus 12:5; Numbers 6:14.

85. RB 19:7.

86. RB 58:7.

87. Saint Basil wrote a Rule for the members of the monastery he founded about 356 on the banks of the Iris in Cappadocia. Before founding a community, Saint Basil visited Egypt, Palestine, Coelesyria, and Mesopotamia to observe the life led by the monks in these countries.

88. RB 8.

89. Discretion (or in Latin, *discretionis*) of the abbot in making decisions is found in several verses of the Rule: 2:24; 55:3; 56:2; 64:19.

90. RB prol. 17.

91. RB prol. 19.

92. RB prol. 15.
93. RB prol. 22.
94. Psalm 33[34]:14–15; RB prol. 17.
95. RB prol. 18.
96. RB prol. 18.
97. RB prol. 19.
98. RB prol. 29–32.
99. RB prol. 33.
100. RB prol. 35.
101. According to the *Merriam-Webster* dictionary, *nirvana* is "the final beatitude that transcends suffering, karma, and samsara and is sought especially in Buddhism through the extinction of desire and individual consciousness."
102. RB prol. 40–41.
103. RB prol. 45.
104. RB prol. 46.
105. "The Rule of Saint Benedict was written anywhere between 530 and 560, is not an entirely original document. It depends in great measure on the rules and traditions of Christian monasticism that existed from the fourth century to the time of its writing. Scholars note that rules and writings like those of St. Pachomius (fourth-century Egypt), St. Basil (fourth-century Asia Minor), St. Augustine (fourth- and fifth-century North Africa), Cassian (fifth-century southern Gaul) stand behind Benedict's Rule and at times are clearly evident in the text. The most important source, however, is the *Rule of the Master,* an anonymous rule written two or three decades earlier." From *The Modern Catholic Encyclopedia* (Collegeville, MN: Liturgical Press, 1995), 78–79.

106. RB prol. 47.

107. RB prol. 49.

108. RB prol. 50.

109. RB prol. 50.

110. Sister Juanita Colón, *The Manhattan Psalter: The Lectio Divina of Sister Juanita Colón* (Collegeville, MN: Liturgical Press, 2002).

111. RB prol. 15–17.

112. Confraternity-Douay version (Rockford, IL: Catholic Book Publishing, 1957).

113. RB prol. 17.

114. RB prol. 22–23.

115. See *Early Monastic Rules: The Rules of the Father and the Regula Orientalis,* trans. Carmela Vircillo Franklin and others (Collegeville, MN: Liturgical Press, 1982).

116. The *Rule of the Master* is an anonymous sixth-century collection of monastic precepts. See *The Rule of the Master*, trans. Luke Eberle (Kalamazoo, MI: Cistercian Publications, 1977).

117. "In drawing up its regulations, we hope to set down nothing harsh, nothing burdensome. The good of all concerned, however, may prompt us to a little strictness in order to amend faults and to safeguard love." RB prol. 46–47.

118. On March 21, 1098, the abbot of the thriving Benedictine abbey of Molesme, Robert, led twenty-one of his monks into the inhospitable thickets of Cîteaux [France] to establish a new monastery where they hoped to follow Benedict of Nursia's Rule for Monasteries in all its fullness.

119. See RB 1:13.

120. RB 58:17.

121. RB 1:2.

122. RB 7:55.

123. RB 1:2.

124. RB 1:3.

125. RB 1:4–5.

126. John Cassian (c. 360–433) is a saint of the Roman Catholic Church and the Eastern Orthodox Church. He is known both as one of the "Scythian monks" and as one of the "Desert Fathers." As a young adult, he and a friend traveled to Palestine, where they entered a hermitage near Bethlehem. After a while there, they journeyed to Egypt and visited a number of monastic foundations. Later, Cassian went to Constantinople, where he became a disciple and friend of John Chrysostom, the patriarch of that city. When Chrysostom ran into theological trouble, Cassian was sent to Rome to plead his cause before the Pope. It was possibly when he was in Rome that he accepted the invitation to found an Egyptian-style monastery in southern Gaul, near Marseilles. His foundation, the Abbey of St. Victor, a complex of monasteries for both men and women, was one of the first such institutes in the West, and served as a model for later monastic development. See *John Cassian: The Conferences*, trans. Boniface Ramsey, Ancient Christian Writers no. 57 (New York: Paulist Press, 1997).

127. RB 42:3, 5.

128. Gregory the Great, *The Life of Saint Benedict*, commentary by Adalbert de Vogüé, trans. Hilary Costello and Eoin de Bhaldraithe (Petersham, MA: St. Bede's, 1993), I.7, 11.

129. RB 72:11.

130. *The Life of Saint Benedict*, II.2, 21.

131. RB 1:6–9.

132. RB 4:20.

133. RB 1:10–11.

134. RB 7:55.

135. In the pre-Vatican II monastic life, there were two classifications of monks: lay brothers and choir monks. Although both shared in the work around the monastery, it was the lay brothers who were primarily devoted to supporting the monastery through their labor. The choir monks spent hours in the *Opus Dei* (Divine Office), giving praise to God through their voices. The lay brothers were distinguished by their brown habit and beards. The choir monks wore black scapulars and were shaven. After Vatican II, these classifications ceased, although the lay brothers, if they chose, could continue in that status. Vatican II encouraged all monastics to have a balanced life of work and prayer.

136. Bernard of Clairvaux, *The Steps of Humility and Pride*, trans. M. Ambrose Conway, Cistercian Fathers Series no. 13a (Kalamazoo, MI: Cistercian Publications, 1989), XIV, 42; pp. 70–71.

137. RB 58:17.

138. *Conversatio morum* does not have a direct English equivalent. It can be defined as a conversion of one's behavior as well as a fidelity to the monastic way of life as given in the Rule of Saint Benedict and the constitutions of the Order.

139. "But as we progress in this way of life and in faith, we shall run on the path of God's commandments, our hearts overflowing with the inexpressible delight of love." RB prol. 49.

140. Four primary documents of early Cistercian history are the *Exordium Parvum*, the *Exordium Cistercii*, the *Carta Caritatis*, and the *Vita Prima* of Bernard. The *Exordium Parvum*, written by Saint Stephen Harding, one of the founders of the Cistercian order, describes the desire of the new order (the Cistercians) to "more tenaciously" be lovers of both the place and the observance of the Rule of Saint Benedict. Later in the document is the description of another founder, Alberic. He is described as "a lover of the Rule and the brethren."

141. RB 2:2.

142. RB 2:1.

143. RB 2:6.

144. RB 72:11.

145. *Meditatio* is one of the four movements in the ancient practice of *lectio divina* (spiritual reading). The four movements are *lectio* (reading), *meditatio* (reflection), *oratio* (responding), *contemplatio* (listening to the Holy Spirit). See M. Basil Pennington, *Lectio Divina: Renewing the Ancient Practice of Praying the Scriptures* (New York: Crossroads, 1998).

146. Saint Stephen Harding, one of the founders of the Cistercian Order in 1098.

147. RB 9:4; 12:4; 13:11; 17:8.

148. M. Basil Pennington, "St. Stephen's Letter on the Use of Hymns," in *The Last of the Fathers: The Cistercian Fathers of Twelfth Century, A Collection of Essays* (Still River, MA: St. Bede's, 1983), 19. See also M. Basil Pennington, "Three Early Documents," *Cistercian Studies* 4, no. 2 (1969): 142–58.

149. RB 2:1–3.

150. RB 2:4.

151. RB 2:5.

152. RB 2:12–14; 3:11.

153. Pennington, "The Epistle of Thurstan of York," in *The Last of the Fathers*, 30n22. See also Pennington, "Three Early Documents."

154. "The Epistle of Thurstan of York," 25–26n6.

155. Ibid., 24n3.

156. Ibid., 29n19.

157. Ibid., 29n20.

158. Ibid., 24n4.

159. Ibid., 25n5.

160. RB 2:6–7.

161. RB 2:30–33.

162. RB 48:1.

163. RB 48:8.

164. Paul says that work is a virtue (2 Thess. 3:7–12), and he instructs the Christian to follow his example, directing attention to his own toil-worn hands (Acts 20:34).

165. The church of Our Lady of the Holy Spirit Monastery was constructed with the labor of the monks and direction of a lay foreman, Mr. Leslie Ray. Work began in the late 1940s and was completed by 1961. The dedication of the church was on October 3, 1975, after all debts were paid.

166. RB prol. 4.

167. Abbot Basil speaks of four monks. Father Lawrence Swartz died on September 26, 2005, at age 98. Father Charles Zell died on June 16, 2005, at age 93. Abbot Augustine Moore (abbot of Our Lady of the Holy Spirit Monastery from 1957 to 1984) died on June 5, 2002, at age 90. Father Luke Kot, one of the founders of the

monastery in 1944, was born on August 3, 1911, and continues working at the monastery in the tailor shop and infirmary.

168. RB 31:10. See also RB 32:4.

169. Second Vatican Ecumenical Council, Dogmatic Constitution on the Church *Lumen Gentium*, no. 11.

170. In 1991, Abbot Basil went to assist the monastery of Our Lady of Joy on Lantao Island near Hong Kong. On July 12, 1999, he returned to the United States.

171. Abbot Basil entered Saint Joseph's Abbey in Massachusetts in 1951.

172. RB 48:18.

173. See RB 58.

174. The Transfiguration of Jesus, Matthew 17:1–8 and Mark 9:9–13, is thought to have occurred on Mount Tabor; "Taboric" refers to the Transfiguration.

175. *Nos fecisti ad te et inquietum est cor nostrum donec requiescat in te.* (Thou hast made us for Thyself, O Lord, and our hearts are restless until they rest in Thee.) Saint Augustine in *Confessions*, book 1, chap. 1.

176. Resurrection of Lazarus, John 11.

177. Dogmatic Constitution of the Church *Lumen Gentium* (1964), chap. 7, no. 48. *Catechism of the Catholic Church*, nos. 52, 694, 541, and 759.

178. RB 49:1.

179. RB 15:1–4.

180. RB 49:1–2.

181. RB 48:14–16.

182. See M. Basil Pennington, *Lectio Divina: Renewing the Ancient Practice of Praying the Scriptures* (New York: Crossroad, 1998).

183. RB 48:17–21.
184. RB 48:22–23.
185. RB 58:8.
186. RB 58:10.
187. RB prol. 1.
188. RB 19:7.
189. RB 7:35–39. In chapter five of the Rule on obedience, Benedict instructs, "This very obedience, however, will be acceptable to God and agreeable to men only if compliance with what is commanded is not cringing or sluggish or half-hearted, but free from any grumbling or any reaction of unwillingness" (RB 5:14).
190. RB 72:11.
191. Sext is midday prayers in which a short reading follows the chanting of two psalms.
192. Written about the year 400, the Rule of Saint Augustine is one of the earliest guides for religious life.
193. *Curritur* (hasten; run) is found in the prologue at 13, 22, and 44. *Festinat* (in a hurry) appears in 73:8 of the Rule.
194. RB prol. 50.
195. RB 2:2; 63:13.
196. RB 72:11.

ABOUT PARACLETE PRESS

Who We Are

Paraclete Press is an ecumenical publisher of books and recordings on Christian spirituality. Our publishing represents a full expression of Christian belief and practice—from Catholic to Evangelical, from Protestant to Orthodox.

Paraclete Press is the publishing arm of the Community of Jesus, an ecumenical monastic community in the Benedictine tradition. As such, we are uniquely positioned in the marketplace without connection to a large corporation and with informal relationships to many branches and denominations of faith.

We like it best when people buy our books from booksellers, our partners in successfully reaching as wide an audience as possible.

What We Are Doing

Books

Paraclete Press publishes books that show the richness and depth of what it means to be Christian. Although Benedictine spirituality is at the heart of all that we do, we publish books that reflect the Christian experience across many cultures, time periods, and houses of worship.

We publish books that nourish the vibrant life of the church and its people—books about spiritual practice, formation, history, ideas, and customs.

We have several different series of books within Paraclete Press, including the best-selling Living Library series of modernized classic texts; A Voice from the Monastery—giving voice to men and women monastics about what it means to live a spiritual life today; award-winning literary faith fiction; and books that explore Judaism and Islam and discover how these faiths inform Christian thought and practice.

Recordings

From Gregorian chant to contemporary American choral works, our music recordings celebrate the richness of sacred choral music through the centuries. Paraclete is proud to distribute the recordings of the internationally acclaimed choir Gloriæ Dei Cantores, who have been praised for their "rapt and fathomless spiritual intensity" by *American Record Guide*, and the Gloriæ Dei Cantores Schola, which specializes in the study and performance of Gregorian chant. Paraclete is also the exclusive North American distributor of the recordings of the Monastic Choir of St. Peter's Abbey in Solesmes, France, long considered to be a leading authority on Gregorian chant performance.

Learn more about us at our Web site:
www.paracletepress.com,
or call us toll-free at
1-800-451-5006.

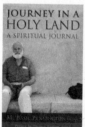